THE NO. 1 SECRET OF THRIVING YOUR LEADERSHIP INFLUENCE

THE ABC METHOD FOR HIGH IMPACT SPEAKING AND PRESENTING

DR AMAT TAAP MANSHOR

PARTRIDGE

Copyright © 2020 by Dr Amat Taap Manshor.

Library of Congress Control Number:		2020919370
ISBN:	Hardcover	978-1-5437-6072-9
	Softcover	978-1-5437-6071-2
	eBook	978-1-5437-6116-0

All rights reserved. No part of this book may be used or reproduced by any means, graphic, electronic, or mechanical, including photocopying, recording, taping or by any information storage retrieval system without the written permission of the author except in the case of brief quotations embodied in critical articles and reviews.

Because of the dynamic nature of the Internet, any web addresses or links contained in this book may have changed since publication and may no longer be valid. The views expressed in this work are solely those of the author and do not necessarily reflect the views of the publisher, and the publisher hereby disclaims any responsibility for them.

Print information available on the last page.

To order additional copies of this book, contact
Toll Free +65 3165 7531 (Singapore)
Toll Free +60 3 3099 4412 (Malaysia)
orders.singapore@partridgepublishing.com

www.partridgepublishing.com/singapore

CONTENTS

Synopsis vii
Why I Wrote This Book ix

Chapter 1   Introduction...1
Chapter 2   Why Effective Communication Matters to Leaders? 8
Chapter 3   The Principles of High-Impact Speaking and
            Presenting 18
Chapter 4   Aspiration 26
Chapter 5   Behaviour 58
Chapter 6   Connection 81
Chapter 7   Application of ABC Method for Leaders 98
Chapter 8   Personal Development Plan 114
Chapter 9   10 Tips for High-Impact Speaking and Presenting ... 121
Chapter 10 Conclusion 140

SYNOPSIS

Observe the types of communication that you have in the workplace on a daily basis. Most of the time it centres on how you wish to influence others or to persuade them to accept your views on a certain matter. Without a doubt, communication skills are fundamental, specifically for leaders, as it gives them an upper hand when dealing with people from all levels of an organisation.

This book delves into the importance of working towards becoming a high-impact speaker and presenter, what we need to do to achieve this desirable outcome, and how we should go about doing it. The principles of high-impact speaking and presenting is discussed in detail, where the author describes the significance of observing the *ABC Method*, a method that he developed based on his own personal experiences whilst working in various sectors of the industry.

The ABC Method, comprising of three fundamental principles—aspiration, behaviour, and connection—ensures the delivery of highly-impactful speeches and presentations by the speakers in a convincing and confident manner. The author has managed to cover the major aspects of a speaker's preparation in making a speech or presentation by focusing on what works and what does not. Readers are enlightened about the various tips and techniques that they could apply to ensure that not only their content, but also the speakers themselves will be positively remembered for giving impactful presentations.

What is interesting about this book is that the author is telling a story based on his very own, using a practical and workable method that is suitable not only for his own use, but also for others who were like him, i.e., someone who used to lack the courage and confidence to stand up in front of a large crowd, to an experienced trainer and consultant that he is today, talking about the very subject that he was afraid of when he was younger— communication and public speaking!

WHY I WROTE THIS BOOK

My heart was racing. My palms were sweaty. I was trying really hard to stop myself from shaking. The words of Mrs. Shim, my English teacher, kept playing in my mind. 'Amat, I want you to give a special talk about Independence Day at the school assembly next week.'

As an introvert, it was only natural for me to have a panic attack when I heard those words. Up until that point in my life, I had always avoided speaking in front of people; public speaking was definitely a no go! I told myself over and over that I should do it, I could do it, but I fought with my feelings and lost, so much so that I decided not to attend school during the day of the event, citing an 'upset stomach' as my reason of absence. In actual fact, I did have an upset stomach, but one caused by my nervousness to speak in front of my teachers and friends.

The whole time I was at home, I felt miserable because I had let my teacher down. Instead of feeling humbled and honoured that I had been handpicked, I had allowed other negative emotions to take control, causing me to shy away from a wonderful opportunity.

When I returned to school the next day, Mrs. Shim took me aside, and we had a long chat as to why I decided not to make the speech. One particular thing that struck me during our conversation was when she commented, 'You lost the greatest opportunity of your life.'

I maintained much of my reserved personality throughout secondary school. There were times when I wanted so much to share my ideas, but I was worried, and even feared, that other people would judge me for the way I looked, dressed, or spoke—and in the end, I kept everything to myself, causing me to lose out on a number of incredible opportunities.

However, Mrs. Shim's comment had greatly impacted me. I did not know it then, but it proved to be very useful in the following years. It completely changed my perspective about talking in front of people.

At 17, I was offered a scholarship to enrol into a programme at a university. The programme required its students to conduct numerous presentations that were compulsory to pass. Although, at first, I had a lot of reservations and doubted my ability to present in public, I remembered Mrs. Shim's comment, and I promised myself that from that day onwards, I would not miss out on any more opportunities in life.

I went through a very rough period in the first few months at the university as I had to crawl out of my comfort zone, doing things I had feared the most whilst growing up—speaking in public. But I never gave up and pushed on and on. Very soon, I was able to publicly speak with ease and comfort. I breezed through university and enhanced my skills to present my assignments to my lecturers and convinced them with my suggestions and recommendations.

I was lucky to have had the opportunity to break away from my shell. I know there are so many others who are timid and shy like I once was; those who have experienced, are currently experiencing, and may be experiencing something similar in the future—whether in the context of an academic, business or working environment, or even in their everyday lives.

Throughout my professional career, I was lucky to have been involved in various types of communication with different groups and levels of people.

In the earlier years of my career, I held senior executive posts at various multinational organisations which exposed me to a string of duties that involved extensive communication at all levels and in different circumstances. Although I was still a novice at these organisations, I was not afraid to make comments and share ideas with my superiors, with the purpose of improving policies and procedures, encouraging teamwork, and even increasing revenue.

Whilst serving as an academic at a few universities, I had the opportunity of teaching and coaching undergraduate and postgraduate students from different walks of life. On several occasions, I also had the chance to present my research papers locally and abroad.

After my career/professional stint, I went on to lead several organisations as CEO, and this has exposed me to new experiences, such as presenting the organisations' recommendations to board members, industry players, the international community, royalties, dignitaries, ministers, and top government officials.

In my personal venture as an entrepreneur, I was very much involved in presenting my ideas and selling business proposals to my target market. There was no way around it—I had to face my clients and convince them to buy the products and services I offered.

Learning from my own journey, I realise how important effective communication is to leaders. I am a bit sad when some leaders are not able to communicate well and fail to share their messages clearly.

One such case occurred when I attended one of my client's company meetings where there were 200 employees in the room. You could literally feel the buzz and the excitement. Upbeat music was playing in the background, and a slick PowerPoint presentation was spinning, doing action-packed transitions on a big screen. Then the music slowly faded, and the group leader confidently strode to the lectern. In a few short minutes, the energy and enthusiasm in the room were dead; unfortunate victims of a horrible presentation. The speaker stumbled over her words, stared uncomfortably at the audience, and gripped the lectern with white-knuckled hands. Meanwhile, everyone's interest flat-lined. Although this speaker is a leader, she obviously did not present like one. This should never happen.

As I travel around the world, I see leaders at all levels who are absolutely disastrous speakers. If you are in a leadership role, you have got to be able to speak and present clearly. Leaders in any organisation are required to give prepared speeches, direct Q&A sessions, and speak extemporaneously. If you hold such a position but are not great at public speaking, you need help immediately. You may be killing your career as a leader.

There are three major problems many leaders encounter when it comes to presenting and speaking:

1. *Clarity on the Objective of the Presentation.* For every single presentation or speaking engagement, you must have a clear objective of the desired direction, outcome, and achievement you seek to obtain from the process. This will, in turn, guide every move you make towards ensuring that there is complete transparency on the subject matter and that you can effectively deliver the content in the right manner.
2. *Poor Stage Behaviour.* Behaviour refers to how we conduct ourselves when speaking in public. Self-presentation and delivery methods are critical ingredients that will make or break you during your performance. How you carry yourself, depending on whether it is a formal or informal gathering, when you take the stage, it should be in line with the message you seek to pass across. Confidently deliver without distracting them.
3. *Lack of Connection with the Audience.* Connection indicates the actions that bind and unite you with your audience. It refers to your engagement with the audience throughout your

entire performance right from the introductory statement. A good communicator is able to adapt to the mood of the listeners by injecting subtle changes befitting the current atmosphere. This way, they can maintain a bond which will facilitate ease of delivery and reception of the subject matter.

The long and short of it is that clear-cut communication skills contribute towards the success of a leader since you have to be able to fully express yourself to everyone. Being a leader also means you get to lead by example. This includes convincing your team to embrace your vision, understand your objectives, and work together towards helping you achieve your goals.

This can be managed when you forge a connection with them. Are they able to identify with the direction you plan on taking? Do they share your beliefs and goals? These are some of the distinctive aspects of a great bond which is inspired and motivated by faith and trust in leadership. Effective communication is, thus, a feature by which better leaders are identified. It is an art that needs to be learnt to be acquired.

Based on these frustrations and observations, I decided to write this book so as to share my personal journey—more importantly, the challenges I faced and the successes I have achieved. It is my passion to provide assistance in the area of personal development, particularly in improving communication and presentation skills for leaders. After reading this book, I hope I would have given you an insight on the proven methods and approaches to develop speaking and presenting skills in a short period.

Trust me, you will have a strong leverage if you have the ability to communicate with confidence and precision. Think about it: You will be able to express yourself in different manners to ensure your words have the desired impact you need. More importantly, you are able to thrive your leadership influence and open wider and bigger opportunities.

In my personal view, effective communication can increase our value by up to 50%. Apart from that, it will raise our level of confidence, level of influence, and level of success three times.

> *When I was a young boy, I would often refuse to talk to adults and cling to the back of my mother's skirt. As an introverted kid, my mother worried my shyness would become debilitating as I got older—to help try and tackle my shyness, my mother always challenged me.*
> —Richard Branson

Just like Richard Branson, in a way, I too had felt 'challenged' by my teacher's comments that day. I am glad that I accepted the challenge because today I realise that most of my successes were partly due to my ability to generate high-impact communication, particularly in

- increasing my *self-confidence,*
- increasing my level of *influence,*
- providing a high level of *clarity,*
- gaining a high level of *trust and respect* from others,
- obtaining a high level of *satisfaction, self-fulfilment, and motivation,*
- increasing *self-value,* and
- generating continuous *wealth.*

I strongly believe that everyone has the ability and opportunity to excel in public speaking. What makes us transform from becoming the worst to the best is our determination to change, learn, and act. With the right techniques and continuous efforts, you will be able to speak and present with confidence.

The best investment that you could do is invest in yourself. Improving your public speaking ability increases professional value by 50% instantly. —Warren Buffett

This book is written based on my personal experience of over 20 years in various positions and levels of responsibilities both in the local and international environments. I have also shared some of the best practices based on my research, observations, and sharing by several experts in the field.

Whether you need to present a business proposal, conduct training, emcee an event, sell a product, convince your colleagues in a meeting, undergo a job interview, or present in conferences, I am positive that the best practices shared in this book will be applicable to various types of speaking formats and situations.

> *Picture yourself in a living room having a chat with your friends. You would be relaxed and comfortable talking to them, the same applies when public speaking.*
> —Richard Branson

In the chapters that follow, I have elaborated the principles of high-impact speaking and presenting that I consistently practise to deliver impactful presentations. I call it my *ABC Method*, which stands for aspiration, behaviour, and connection. I will take you through the 'why,' 'how,' and 'what' of each principle, and at the end of the day, I hope that what I have shared, including some of my life-journey stories, will assist you in coming up with your very own highly-impactful personal development plan.

I am thrilled to take you along this journey, and I hope that what I have shared here will help you in your quest to improve your communication skills and making them your top priority. Once you have mastered the art of high-impact speaking, there is no turning back.

All the best, and enjoy your transformation journey! Remember, 'impossible' is just a word.

> *Impossible is just a big word thrown around by small men who find it easier to live in the world they've been given than to explore the power they have to change it. Impossible is not a fact. It's an opinion. Impossible is not a declaration. It's a dare. Impossible is potential. Impossible is temporary. Impossible is nothing.*
> —Muhammad Ali

CHAPTER 1

Introduction

The small packed meeting room was silent. Everyone had their eyes glued on him.

He removed his blazer and tie and started folding the sleeves of his shirt. They nervously watched as he furiously started typing on his cell phone.

Suddenly, he looked up at them with a big grin on his face. 'I've just ordered pizza for us, it's going to be a long night!'

The atmosphere in the room was relaxed. Despite an extremely tight project deadline to meet in several hours, everyone was in a calm state of mind. Their CEO had decided to stay back at the office in the wee hours of the morning, drinking stale coffee and eating cold pizza together with them.

The CEO's presence in the room had greatly impacted his employees for the very reason that he did not even have to be there. Throughout the night, he communicated his thoughts to them, shared his concerns, and made some recommendations, all the time motivating and providing guidance to his employees to push ahead and complete the pending project.

What the CEO has done here might seem rather trivial; however, in fulfilling his role as a leader, he has managed to create a big impact by focusing on maintaining excellent communication with his employees in getting through a challenging moment.

Now let me start by giving you some scenarios.

Have you ever been afraid of being singled out—in class or at work—to present an idea to your friends and colleagues? Have you ever experienced the fear of being ridiculed or criticised? Have you ever felt so embarrassed standing in front of an audience that the only thing you could do was to freeze in terror?

Perhaps, time and time again, you have wished that your fear, embarrassment, and agony of speaking in public would just go away.

Have you ever listened to a speech so powerful that it sent shivers down your spine? Have you ever been thoroughly mesmerised by a speaker that you did not realise the hours that have gone by? Have you ever felt so much energy that has been passed from the speaker to the audience members?

And perhaps you secretly wished that you had the qualities of such a speaker?

Regardless of the scenarios you may have encountered above, do not fret because you are not alone! Believe it or not, communication skills are considered one of the most dreaded and feared skills, so much so that even powerful people in the world, such as successful entrepreneurs, famous celebrities, and even presidents and prime ministers of countries, also harbour insecurities when it comes to public speaking.

Like it or not, you have to face the fear, as this is the best way of conquering the fear itself. Strengthening your communication skills will elevate you to a higher level—you will not only achieve greater heights, but you will also be appreciated and respected.

How is this possible, you may ask. Well, with better communication, you will not have any hesitations in articulating your thoughts. You will know how to express yourself, how to manage your facial expressions and body language, and how to even deal with the audience's emotions. Having good communication skills also improves your relationship with others as you will be able to connect with them on different levels, depending on the circumstances of the case.

This book is based on my very own journey, from the shy and timid boy that I was to the confident person I am today. I have learnt that it is never too late to learn, to relearn, and to improve our communication skills. If we choose to shy away from opportunities, we will definitely lose out in life.

Whether you are an introvert or extrovert, or whether you are a born communicator or otherwise, after reading this book, I am confident it will improve your communication skills and, ultimately, turn you into a highly influential and impactful leader.

The approach of this book is simple. I find that one of the easiest ways of understanding something is by asking questions. However, it is not simply about questioning; it is about asking the right questions to get the right answers. Each chapter in this book breaks down three important questions that begin with *why*, *how*, and *what*. Two critical ingredients are the person's self-presentation and delivery methods, for example, *why* you should learn the skills, *how* you should apply the skills, and *what* you should do to sharpen the skills. This approach is important so that you may be able to appreciate and apply what you have learnt to your full advantage. All best practices shared in this book are based on real-life examples and experiences for you to use and get instant results. At the end of every main topic, you will find "Put Yourself in Practice" which allow you to immediately practise or reinforce certain skills. I also share some of my personal stories that relate to the practices of high-impact communication skills, particularly on public speaking and conducting presentations.

Chapter 2 of this book discusses why effective presentation and communication matters to leaders. To be successful as a leader, you need to have the ability to inspire others around you and to drive them to believe in your vision, in your deliverables, and in your desired outcomes. Many leaders have excellent ideas; however, they fail to become a source of inspiration, and because of this shortfall, they are unable to properly convey significant messages and issues of concern. It is, therefore, crucial for leaders to acquire public speaking skills to enable them to effectively communicate to the respective target audience.

Chapter 3 of this book discusses the principles of high-impact speaking and presenting. I have come to realise and observe, throughout my professional experience of over 20 years, that I had been consistently practising some principles which have helped me in delivering highly-impactful presentations. These principles were used, and are still used, every time I speak and present to my audience, and the results have been steadily positive. For the past three years, I have made further research on each principle, and it has become very clear to me that for us to produce highly-impactful public speaking and presentation skills, we need to master and practise three principles: aspiration, behaviour, and connection. I call this my ABC Method. As simple as ABC might sound, these principles can only work if they are accurately applied.

Chapter 4 discusses the first principle of my ABC Method, which is aspiration. I strongly believe that before we can get anything to even happen, we have to hope and have a strong desire for it. We need to know what we want from the very beginning instead of starting blindly and ending up going in circles. Aspiration refers to the concept of 'beginning with an end in mind.' This simply means that each time we begin each day, task, or project, we do that with a clear aim of our direction and desired outcome. To produce continuous high-impact results, we must have clarity on why we are doing it, how we want to deliver it, and what we need to do to consistently maintain highly-impactful results. Most importantly, when speaking or presenting to your audience, you must be able to relate your aspirations with them.

Chapter 5 discusses the second principle in my ABC Method, which is behaviour. How we behave whilst speaking and presenting is extremely critical to gain the interest and trust of our audience. This chapter looks at how we need to present ourselves, specifically, our personality and appearance, to our audience. Once you are out there in the limelight, every little thing is crucial: eye contact, facial expressions, body language. Putting your hands in your pockets, pacing back and forth, or even excessive hand gestures could mean you are nervous. If we are uncomfortable with our behaviour, our audience will also achieve the same feeling. Because of this behaviour, the messages carried in our presentation could sometimes be misconstrued or misunderstood. Behaviour, therefore, refers to the way we conduct ourselves when we speak and present to our audience. The chapter also elaborates two critical ingredients: self-presentation and method of delivery. High-impact behaviour produces an effective and persuasive action so that you may have full control over yourself, subsequently creating a high level of confidence and reducing anxiety.

Chapter 6 discusses the third principle, which is connection. In this chapter, I provide tips on how to connect with the audience, and I provide several examples that could be used to get a productive session. Picture this: You have done fantastic research about your topic, and you are all hyped up to present to your audience. Unfortunately, the moment you stand in front your audience, you start the journey on your own, with little regard to your audience. What makes it worse is that you are unaware of their expressions; some might be bored, others might be confused, or they are not even concentrating on your presentation. The key here is connection. Connection refers to the action that binds and unites you with the audience. It is all about how we engage with our audience throughout our presentation. We should be physically, psychologically, and emotionally connected with our audience so that there is a high level of trust, which, in turn, creates a wealth of opportunities. Thus, the element of connection is significant towards producing a long-lasting impact on your audience.

Chapter 7 discusses the application of ABC Method for speakers and trainers. As much as theories are important for us to understand how to produce highly-impactful public speaking and presentation skills, we need to ensure that we can effectively apply them when we speak and present in front of a live audience. This is an important chapter, as it illustrates how best a speaker and trainer can apply the ABC Method in the course of their speaking and presentation engagements.

In chapter 8, I offer some tips on how you can come up with a workable 'personal development plan' and how it can be utilised to support your dreams of becoming an influential and impactful leader through your highly-effective presentation. It is important for us to have an action plan as we will actually know what we are doing and we can keep track of our achievements. This is why the personal development plan needs to be a dynamic document that is regularly reviewed to ensure that it is an effective, accurate, and relevant plan.

How do you get your audience to pay attention to you when you speak? How do you get your message across to them so that they are able to grasp the important outcomes that you have shared? These questions can easily be answered after reading Chapter 9 - 10 Tips for High-Impact Speaking and Presenting as it will provide you with some effective tips on how to deal with the above and other related situations. These tips have been tested; however, for them to effectively work, you will need to put in a lot of hard work and frequent practice.

Finally, chapter 10 is the summary and conclusions of all the previous chapters, including recommendations on the way forward. It is my hope that you will be able to apply the new knowledge and skills in the best way possible to ensure that you achieve your dream of becoming a highly-impactful speaker and presenter.

Having effective communication skills will definitely broaden your opportunities and eventually increase your leadership value. Try it, and you will see what I mean.

> *If you've never tried, how will you ever know if there's any chance?*
> —Jack Ma.

CHAPTER 2

Why Effective Communication Matters to Leaders?

Leadership is about having a vision. However, having a vision is only half the battle. Leaders have way more responsibility than just having a vision; having a vision is one thing, whilst communicating that vision to the team is another. Therefore, as a leader, if you want to succeed, you need to be able to present your vision in a way that inspires and drives others to help you achieve it, especially during turbulent times. Your presentation skills, or how you communicate, are not only extremely important but also very critical in getting positive results. Generally, a leader spends at least 75-90% of his or her time communicating.

The findings further argue that 'everything a leader does to influence others involves communicating' and 'good communication skills are the foundation of effective leadership.' Ideally, as a leader, these are some of the best practices you should focus on first when it comes to nurturing your leadership and communication skills. It is only after you have mastered effective communication that you should think of advancing to attributes such as higher-level team and strategic skills that are more readily considered leadership skills. Showing up and communicating one-on-one to direct reports or your employees, shareholders, or other external stakeholders is very critical to selling a vision and even stamping leadership. As a leader, you must make sure your presentation skills are competent enough to ensure that the message you are delivering resonates appropriately according to the current situation in your organisation.

When we think about leadership, we usually picture political leaders who stand at podiums rallying crowds to support their causes, or athletes who spur their teams to push their limits and try harder, or executives who develop strategies to help their colleagues edge out the competition. However, in real life, leaders wear many hats and bear many responsibilities. For example, leaders help others do the right things, drive innovation and change, as well as build a new vision for a greater future for all. Following the vast responsibility that leaders carry on their shoulders, being dynamic, exciting, and inspiring are must attributes that leaders need to learn if, at all, they want to impact their organisations.

A study by Sunnie Giles published in *Harvard Business Review* states that one of the absolute most important leadership skills from around the world is the ability to communicate clearly with others.

One of the essential qualities that have been emphasised throughout this study is the fact that leaders must be effective communicators, a core reason why public speaking is important for leadership in any kind of setting. Therefore, if you want to be a leader within your organisation, you must be an excellent communicator, and to do so must abide by the three Cs,' namely leaders challenge, encourage change, and connect.

Leaders challenge. Public speaking on most occasions is more about challenging people's perception of something than just about introducing new ideas. Public speaking focuses more on challenging yourself and developing the confidence to speak in public. Anyone who has ever attempted to stand in front of a group of strangers and talked for just half an hour knows how intimidating it can be, especially if it is his or her first time talking to a group of people. Therefore, it takes more than a nerve of steel to be a public speaker. However, when you *challenge yourself to speak in front of an audience* over and over, this increases your confidence, thus helping you manage stage fright.

Building confidence eventually leads to self-belief, which, in turn, makes it easier for you to face other challenges in your business life, such as innovating new products or services and even approaching new business partners. When you eventually become effective at challenging your audience's ideas, then you have the power to challenge your team members' opinions, their abilities, and the direction of the company. In all honesty, becoming a leader is challenging; thus, any aspiring leader must invest in personal development to overcome communication challenges.

Leaders encourage change. The art of persuasion is not only crucial in the business world but also the world of public speaking. Whereas challenging an opinion is the first step towards bringing change, making that real and lasting change is a different story altogether. Moving forward, encouraging change is the *how* part of leadership. If, for example, you challenge a colleague to change their mind about something and you become successful, the next step towards helping that colleague change completely lies in showing him or her how to create lasting change. This means teaching him or her a new way of thinking, doing, and/or being.

Great public speakers do not just talk; they teach. They ensure that each audience member has a new tool he or she can use to change his or her life or business for the better. The tool could be something as simple as instructing business owners on *how* to use social media more effectively or something as profound as teaching recovering addicts *how* to stay committed to their new goals. Encouraging change is a high-prized skill, both at the podium and in a staff meeting. If you have enough self-awareness to know you are not the greatest at teaching or instructing others, signing up for public speaking events can develop this much-needed skill.

Leaders connect. One of the main things you will learn about being an effective public speaker is to share your humanity. Audience members do not latch onto ideas so much as they latch onto people. For many public speakers, when just starting, they try to be *perfect* instead of *authentic*. And what happens when you focus on being perfect? You come across as stiff and robotic. This happens especially when you try so hard not to mess up. However, in the process of being perfect, mistakes happen. The same thing can happen to new leaders, especially when they try so hard to be 'leaders' to a certain extent or to help the people around them become better.

To be an effective public speaker and leader, you have to focus on connecting with the people you are trying to lead and inspire. If you speak to people in a way that is transparent and authentic, you will bring about change and innovation. The best part is when you decide to stop focusing on being perfect or authoritative and start focusing on being human and connecting with fellow human beings. By doing so, you will be amazed at how many people would want to communicate with you. If you are currently a leader within your organisation or hope to be one in the future, we encourage you to follow this advice and identify how public speaking can help you develop the communication skills you need to lead effectively.

Majority of the leaders today are often evaluated by their abilities to speak effectively. If you listen to effective leaders, one of the skills they possess is their ability to speak in public. Becoming a better speaker is both a learnt skill and an art. Most of the best leaders today were not good public speakers at the beginning of their careers. Unlike reading and writing, public speaking is not one of those necessary skills taught during our school years. However, public speaking is about practising to be you and mustering the courage to stand in front of people and connect with them naturally.

The more you put yourself out there speaking and practising speaking effectively, the more you should work towards improving your public speaking skills. Knowing your tone and what to say are the most crucial aspects of public speaking. If you are an aspiring public speaker, it is vital to learn that with the right tools and guidance, you can become a better speaker. It is just a matter of coming out, learning from previous mistakes, and growing better along the way.

Based on my many years of being in leadership roles, I have learnt that communication skills come across as the pillar for any great leader in society. One of the questions that keep popping up in my mind is whether someone can be a good leader without communication skills. The concern for effective communication further pushes me to imagine how a leader can connect, involve, arouse, and provoke people if he or she cannot communicate a vision. Therefore, it is essential to note that excellent communication skills are at the centre of human life. Everything we engage in/with demand communication in one way or the other. Issues such as dealing with customer complaints, customer service, solving challenges, and initiating change, all require effective communication.

In my view, I firmly believe that a good leader should possess some of the following attributes: the art of persuasion, responsibility, and proper management skills to motivate his or her team to deliver set-out goals. Elements such as planning, monitoring, and the ability to communicate go a long way in encouraging performance amongst teams and employees. Overall, a leader must be able to communicate clearly to help his or her organisation achieve the overall business objectives.

I have realised that majority of leaders suffer from what is called career blunders simply because they do not take communication skills as seriously as they should. Many of these leaders pay more attention to other aspects of their jobs to the extent of ignoring the communication factor in their overall performance. Whilst majority of leaders ignore communication, great leaders work towards developing their communication with others. In fact, no single person can carry out different functions in an organisation by himself or herself, and oftentimes knowing the power of effective communication comes to the rescue when dealing with a team or even the top management.

Leadership and proper communication come across as the primary needed expertise in any organisation because they play a significant role in managing people. A good leader knows when and how to communicate with his or her team or employees to get them to perform their duties effectively. The ability to communicate clearly and precisely enables a leader to convey the message without losing the message. Maintaining good relationships and forging future relationships as well as opportunities, all begin with proper communication.

Knowing when and how to communicate with different groups of people in an organisation goes a long way in helping the organisation achieve its goals in the marketplace. Top management, in particular, plays a significant role in facilitating different departments in the organisation. Therefore, communicating helps in ensuring that each department is well equipped to perform its duties in the organisation effectively.

For one to be a great leader, he or she must learn to communicate. Inspirational leaders are touted in the marketplace as great speakers who have significant values that aim at empowering others. Overall, teams follow and appreciate a leader by his or her ability to communicate important information clearly in a language that can be understood by all.

Exceptional communication skills are not only necessary for any leader but also mandatory when managing employees and conveying anticipations on assigned responsibilities. A leader must be able to communicate his or her thoughts easily and at the same time inspire the people he or she is leading. The success of an organisation primarily anchors on the ability of a leader to communicate and create inclusivity amongst the workforce.

The question of why leaders should develop critical communication skills is well answered in the following tips:

- In a highly interactive world, majority of top management leaders and managers spend most of their time talking to different groups of people. The fact that a higher percentage of time is spent in communication with others underscores the role of communication in business. The introduction of different communication devices and tools, such as mobile phones, social media, and messaging apps, have all contributed to increased interaction amongst leaders. For that reason, leaders have no choice but to sharpen their communication skills to keep up with the increasing communication needs.
- Proper communication skills play a significant role in creating a climate of mutual understanding between a leader and his or her followers. The message reaches the people it is intended to in the most precise and straightforward manner, thus making teams deliver their duties significantly. Therefore, managers who aspire to become great leaders in the future have no choice but to learn effective communication and its role in uniting and creating followership.
- The value of excellent communication skills in a workplace not only creates understanding and belief amongst people but also provokes them to implement the principles and traits their leader wants them to model.
- The overall performance of the people involved with a particular organisation frequently depends on the type of

leadership in place and the manner of communication style implemented by the leader. The role of leadership is all about nurturing positive relationships between top management and the workforce. Therefore, leaders need to master communication skills for the sake of the people they lead.

- Day-to-day business transactions require excellent communication skills from leaders. Solving problems and making decisions come across as core duties of leadership. Therefore, communication is at the centre of all primary functions of an organisation, whether a leader wants to acknowledge it or not. Performance in the organisation imitates the communication strengths of a leader. For example, effective communication results in strong relationships amongst employees, whilst poor communication results in misunderstandings and poor relationships.
- It is the responsibility of leaders to provide regular feedback to employees based on their behaviour and performance. However, how well a leader communicates determines the way employees receive the message. Therefore, a leader's communication is in direct proportion with how employees behave and perform their duties. When the conversation is clear and concise, employees not only carry out their duties effectively but also improve their behaviour at the workplace.
- Effective teams in an organisation are built on excellent communication skills. The ability of a leader to set rules, define roles, and make decisions helps in attaining targets. Employee motivation, productivity, and inclusivity in an organisation are also achieved with excellent communication skills.
- A leader should always strive to be understood and ensure that the message he or she intends to communicate get to the recipient as envisioned by the leader. It is only when the message is clear that aspects such as innovation, identification of problems, and mastery of goals are made possible.

- Research findings have again shown that effective communication results in overall company performance and improvement. In addition, high-performing employees were also discovered to have interacted with significant proper communication from their leaders, which influenced their high performance.
- As a leader, your communication can be a crucial tool for shaping the attitudes and behaviours of your employees. For business goals to be achieved as intended, employees always seek for direction and expectations from their leaders. Once employees understand what is expected of them, they are willing to go out of their way to meet their expectations. Excellent communication not only ensures that employees know what to do but also the type of behaviour they need to model to meet the expectations of the organisation.
- It is essential to point out here that the cost of poor communication is high. Poor communication not only cost organisations money but also results in loss of lives, opportunities, and competitive advantage in industries. As a leader, this is a nightmare you do not need to deal with because every failure is a representation of a wrong decision.

For any organisation to remain effective, leadership is seen as an essential factor in ensuring the success and relevancy of the organisation's operation. Through leadership and supervision, the organisation's goals can be achieved as long as the leader has the skill it provides and the capability to initiate structure as well as clear directions for subordinates to perform their tasks effectively. Leadership in an organisation plays a significant role in offering guidance and positioning the organisation for success.

Ultimately, effective leadership is the backbone of any organisation. Leaders must have the ability to inspire their teams and workforce to act in a manner that aligns with the overall work culture of the organisation. Facilitating important functions and duties in the organisation calls for leaders not only to be inspirational but also act in selfless ways for the sake of their people. A leader who is equipped with effective communication skills has the ability to inspire both employees and investor confidence in the organisation.

Therefore, if communication skills are the most crucial skill in the better performance of both people and the organisation, now is the best time for a leader to invest in excellent communication skills. The journey towards gaining effective communication skills is not going to be easy. However, with practice, continued learning, and integration into the daily routine of the work culture, a leader would be able to master the skills and eventually result in effective communication to the team and top management.

CHAPTER 3

The Principles of High-Impact Speaking and Presenting

3.1 Speaking and Presenting? What Is That?

Speaking and presenting remain a driving force in our daily lives because humans continue to rely on spoken words when dealing and connecting with one another. Spoken words are used to inform, influence, and impact us in many different ways, so much so that there is grave importance in getting our words out right.

Saying the wrong thing, or saying the right thing in the wrong manner, or not saying it at all, these will all have a profound effect on the way we connect with everyone else in the world.

Let us not get too excited here. Instead of thinking how you are going to connect with people around the world, let us start by focusing on how you are going to connect with your audience when you stand in front of them to speak.

Will fear start creeping in? Will you get nauseous? Will you faint?

Or will you face them with a smug? With arrogance? With haughtiness?

No to all the above, of course.

Speaking and presenting are an act where you perform your speech to a live audience. It is a skill that can be developed and enhanced and, once you have acquired it, will inevitably transform you into a person with high confidence.

3.2 Why Speaking and Presenting Are Important to You?

If you are successful in speaking and presenting, it will certainly open up a lot of prospects and opportunities for you.

One thing is for certain: Speaking and presenting improve your personal development because when you give speeches and presentations, your personal satisfaction increases whenever a good speech or presentation is made. You will have more confidence, and your anxiety will reduce, especially when your audience gives you a positive and favourable response.

The more speeches and presentations you make, the more you will enjoy the experience and the more you will want to speak. Your credibility will be enhanced, and you are also able to express yourself better to your audience and to the people around you. This is important as your communication and interaction will improve, and you will find that it is easy to connect with people from all levels.

Because you have been exposed to public speaking, your critical thinking skills and interpersonal skills will be enhanced. Not only that, but your creativity and professionalism will also be elevated, and this will undoubtedly help you with career advancements as they are valuable skills which are required for the job market.

Let me give you an example.

Let us assume there are two junior executives in an organisation, A and B.

Although both are performers, Junior Executive A has taken the initiative to take up courses in speaking and presenting. Because of this, she has been conducting great presentations, and her superior has taken notice of her improvement.

Now wouldn't you say that Junior Executive A is at an advantage compared with Junior Executive B?

3.3 Types of Speakers

Generally, there are four types of speakers. You may be able to identify these types with some speakers you know:

a. The Avoider

'There was no contact at all from the speaker. He/She was either looking down at his/her notes or staring at the ceiling and walls. It was as though he/she hated the sight of us!'

When it is time for Avoiders to present to their audience, they will do everything it takes to avoid facing them. They make no eye contact with the audience, their body language is cold, and they seem almost acting distant.

b. The Resister

'The speaker seemed a bit odd to me. He/She has great content, and his/her audiovisuals were fantastic. It really looked like he/she had done a lot of work on his/her preparation. However, the downside was he/she seemed really, really reluctant to speak. Kind of spoiled the entire presentation.'

Resisters are those who are afraid to speak in public, but because they do not have a choice, they still speak; however, they do so with great reluctance.

c. The Accepter

'The speaker did quite an okay job, but I felt that he/she could have presented better. Something was missing."

The Accepter is someone who is able to do presentations but does not look and/or feel enthusiastic about them.

Occasionally, Accepters can be quite persuasive when they speak, and the audience will feel satisfied with their performance.

d. The Seeker

'So much passion and enthusiasm from him/her. He's/she's a world-class speaker!'

The Seeker always looks for opportunities to speak, and when they finally speak, they are extremely poised and confident.

Seekers take extra steps to work on their speaking and presentation skills, and they are not afraid to explore new areas and take on challenges.

3.4 High-Impact Speaking and Presenting

I believe, over the years, you have had the opportunity to listen to various speakers with their respective speaking styles.

Why is it that some of these speakers are stuck in your mind, whilst you cannot recall some others?

Why is it that some speakers have impacted you in a way so great that you have changed your ways to improve based on the recommendations made by the speakers?

And why is it that you feel you have wasted your time, effort, or money listening in to some speakers who have failed to make any impact during their speech?

Several basic principles need to be considered to make one a good speaker or presenter.

First and foremost, good speakers pay a lot of attention to their audience. They take time and effort to ensure that their presentations are catered to the audience's needs. Often dull presentations are conducted by speakers who fail to see the importance of respecting the audience.

When speaking to an audience, it is important to address their needs and meet their expectations. In this case, the audience is there to listen to you speak, and they need to understand what you are talking about. As a speaker, you should not be 'the boss' in the room; rather, you are someone who is relaying messages to your audience in the manner that they feel comfortable with.

The audience must have a sense of understanding about what you are talking about. Check your audience's background before speaking to them for you to know the purpose of their being there. Find out who they are and what their age ranges are. Do they come from various backgrounds, or are they all within the same category of people?

Some speakers skip this step because they believe that the audience should adapt to their style and presentation. However, what good will it be if the speaker is the only one who understands what he is saying?

The presentation, as a whole, should not be too exhausting. Notwithstanding certain type of content which may be heavy, the presentation should be a relaxing one where, at the end of it, the audience gets the message that the speaker has put across.

It is advisable to find a common ground and bond with the audience. Impactful speakers are able to bring the audience along in their journey, sharing their stories and insights so that the audience is left with a memorable and inspirational experience.

Your audience will appreciate if you share stories of your personal struggles and achievements as they could then relate to you. Eventually, they will have a deeper connection to you and trust you more.

3.5 My Personal Experience

To date, I have had over 20 years of experience in public speaking and presenting. I have made several observations during this particular time, and I realised that because of my consistency in putting several principles to practice, I have managed to deliver high-impact speaking and presenting sessions to different varieties of audience.

I would like to share these principles with you—I call them my ABC Method, which stands for Aspiration, Behaviour, and Connection. I have made my own research on each principle, and I strongly believe that I have managed to substantially deliver key messages to my audiences when I adopt my ABC Method.

If you look at the diagram below, you can see how interconnected they are with one another. This means that you need all three to make it work. Achieving one or two principles whilst neglecting the others will not lead you towards becoming a high-impact speaker and presenter.

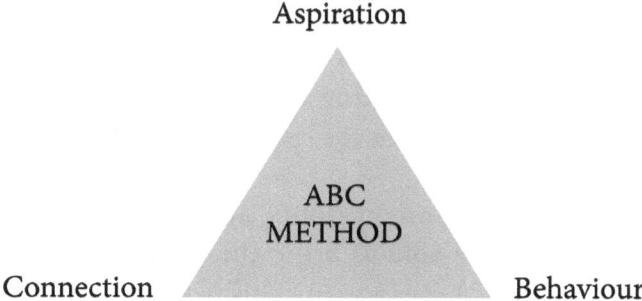

I have used the ABC Method consistently and continuously throughout my experience as a speaker and presenter, and the results have been positive. I use it whenever I speak to small, medium, or large audiences, whether in conferences or small coaching and training sessions. I have also applied it when I conduct presentations to different people, from my office colleagues right up to high-profile officers and government ministers.

Each principle will be further elaborated in the upcoming chapters, but let me give you a brief idea what each principle means:

a. **Aspiration**

By definition, aspiration is a strong desire to achieve something high or great. When I speak of aspiration, I am referring to the concept of 'beginning with an end in mind.'

What this means is that for every single task or project that you take on every day, you must have a clear aim of the desired direction, outcome, and achievement.

It may seem easy theoretically; however, in reality, things may not work in your favour.

For example, let us assume that you begin a task at work without even considering what you plan to achieve. What do you think will happen along the way? Undoubtedly, you will not know what to expect because you are blindly executing the task without knowing what the desired outcome is.

To produce continuous high-impact results, we must have clarity on *why* we are doing a particular task, i.e., the purpose of our intention; *how* we want to deliver the task; and *what* should we do to make us consistently maintain the same high-impact results.

Similarly, when speaking and presenting, you need to have a clear purpose, and this translates to your aspiration, i.e., what you intend to achieve at the end of your session. Most importantly, this aspiration should be one that can be deeply connected with your audience's aspiration as well.

b. Behaviour

Behaviour refers to how we conduct ourselves when we speak in public. Self-presentation and delivery methods are the critical ingredients that will make or break you during your performance.

As a high-impact speaker and presenter, you have high-impact behaviour instilled in you. This will then allow you to have full control over your emotions and, consequently, will increase your confidence level and reduce your anxieties. High-impact behaviour will develop and further strengthen your persuasion skills, which is a significant advantage when you need to attract your audience's attention.

c. Connection

Connection indicates the actions that bind and unite you with your audience. It refers to your engagement with the audience throughout your performance.

A strong connection with your audience allows them to feel at ease with you. As a high-impact speaker and presenter, you are physically, psychologically, and emotionally connected with your audience, making them trust you and the messages that you are relaying to them.

CHAPTER 4

Aspiration

4.1 Introduction

> *To understand the heart and mind of a person, look not at what he has already achieved, but at what he aspires to.*
>
> —Kahlil Gibran

What does aspiration really mean, and why do I think that it is one of the most critical elements to become a high-impact speaker and presenter?

Imagine this scenario: You are driving along a road, but you do not have a destination in mind. You are driving aimlessly without a particular purpose, and at the end of the ride, you have spent considerable time, money, and effort on a task that have led you to no particular end.

Why do we make this drive without any particular purpose in mind when we could have better planned what our destination could have been in the first place?

Just like how it is in real life, setting our destination is an invaluable step that we should take when we are working towards getting something. There are struggles that we constantly face in our lives, specifically with regard to achieving our goals. We may feel that we are progressing forward; however, without having a clear direction and destination, our journey ahead undeniably becomes harder; hence, beginning your journey with a clear purpose in mind is something that should be desired.

4.2 Clarity

In a world full of distractions, it is easy for us to lose the sense of clarity that we need to remain focused and resolute.

Distractions can come in many shapes and sizes. You may think that distractions only come from the outside, but internal distractions are much harder to overcome.

Let me explain further.

There are various types of external distractions, but let us pick the most common ones, particularly in the workplace. How many can you think of? Some of the usual ones include social media, phone usage, or maybe even a noisy office caused by one or two (or more) chatty colleagues.

I can assure you that it is not an easy task to overcome external distractions such as the above, but the advantage to this is that they are all existing externally and not within you. This means that it is much easier for you to either 'leave' or 'stop' or 'ignore' these distractions to suit your needs and expectations.

But how do we deal with distractions that exist within us?

When you were a child, do you remember the things that would distract your focus in something? They are mostly external distractions caused by what you see or hear or feel.

However, as you grow older, there are many other personal and professional distractions that exist internally.

As you age, you find that your focus, needs, and expectations in life have changed. Things that may interest you before could have now dwindled, and likewise, you will find that you have more questions to answer, more issues to address, and more challenges to surpass. You will face internal distractions that you have never faced before as a child.

This is the point in time where clarity plays a vital role in your life.

4.2.1 Why Do You Need Clarity?

Clarity is essential because it clears your mind and allows you to take responsibilities for all your actions in a detailed and focused manner.

As you progress in life, it is very important for you to manage the distractions that come your way to allow you to pave your way smoothly ahead.

You only have so much time and energy, and the last thing you want to do is be unnecessarily burdened by agitations and upsets caused by internal and external distractions.

Start decluttering your life and your mind—only allow important things to remain and get rid of those that will only impede your journey to achieve your goals. You will feel relieved when you have done this exercise. It will be a weight off your shoulders!

4.2.2 How Can You Have Clarity?

There are several ways to have clarity in life; however, the first crucial step is to accept that there are distractions around and/or within you. That way, you can easily identify and remove or push them away from your life.

- **Describe Yourself Clearly**

Go all out and fight for clarity if you want it in your life. It all starts from within you, and it will not work if you fail to realise the significance of it.

Have you ever been in a job interview where the interviewer asks you to describe yourself and you sit there blank-faced? It does seem like a simple question, doesn't it? But chances are, if you are unsure about how to describe yourself clearly, it looks like you may have some ambiguities in your life that need to be addressed first.

To have clarity, first and foremost, you need to be able to describe yourself with clarity. Are you the person you think you are or the person you hope you are?

Be completely honest with yourself. You are who you are, and it takes a lot of courage and guts to admit who you really are because the real you might not be someone who has achieved a lot in life.

More importantly, this exercise is for you to know and accept yourself. This is the first step towards having clarity.

- **Describe What You Want to Be**

After you have described yourself clearly, the next step is to describe what you aspire to be. For example, in your current state, you might be an introvert who is afraid of meeting people or communicating your ideas to your superiors at the office. You now need to describe what you want to be, for example, you want to be someone who is extremely confident and sure of himself or herself.

Describing what you want to be is like a wish list. It is something that you do not have today but something that you want to get in time. It might seem like an impossible task, and some pessimistic friends would say that it is something unfeasible. This is why you need to reflect and remove the negative vibes around you. Stay focused as this is an important step towards having clarity in your life.

- **Identify Your Goal/Purpose**

In the process of having clarity, you have to identify your purpose in life and the goals that you want to achieve.

If you are able to clearly describe yourself and what you want to be, the process of identifying your goals will be much easier. Without them, you lack focus and direction, and this may disrupt your process of taking control.

Setting goals will also provide you a benchmark to determine if you are actually making progress or succeeding.

Progressing in life without having a purpose could be an adventurous ride for some; however, if you have already specified what you need to achieve, the journey ahead will not be as tricky!

- **Clear Your Mind and Focus on Your Goal**

Clear your mind from any clutter and work towards achieving your goal.

Let me give you an example. What difference does it make if you drive a car with a full tank of petrol compared with a car that has an empty tank?

I believe you will be driving at ease towards your destination in the former instance as compared with the latter, where your mind will be troubled by many things: Will you make it to your destination? Is there a petrol kiosk nearby? What if your car stops in the middle of the road?

This is what I mean by having a clear mind. Empty the distractions from your mind to plot your goals clearer and move your way ahead with clarity and precision.

4.3 What Do You Need to Do to Have Clarity?

Time and time again, we say that we need clarity in our lives; however, what do we really need to do to have it? Is it something so incomprehensible?

Trust me, it is not. By practising high-impact habits, you will be able to have clarity in your personal and professional lives.

4.3.1 High-Impact Habits

If you have a goal and you want to achieve it, you have to have some habits in place to ensure that it is achievable.

The following are some high-impact habits that I have been practising. Practise them, preach them, and you will certainly live them!

- **Start Each Day on a Positive Note**

When you wake up, say a prayer and smile. In an instant, you will be surrounded by positive vibes. Isn't this a great start to every brand new day?

Be grateful with what you have, and remind yourself to do this every day. You are able to control your thoughts and moods, so it is entirely up to you to make your day a good and positive one.

Either you run the day or the day runs you. —Jim Rohn

- **Do What You Say You Are Going to Do**

Less talk and more action, please! You might be feeling upbeat and energised. You may have a lot of great ideas brimming inside you. But believe me, nothing works if they are all talk.

If you want things to move, to improve, to progress, to actually happen, start doing it. That is how you move ahead in your journey towards achieving your goals.

- **End Each Day Without a Grudge**

It is very important to have a good finish at the end of the day because it will affect how you start your day the next morning. If you end your day with bitterness, you will not be in the right mood or frame of mind when you wake up.

It is not easy to have a good ending each day because there may be trying and exasperating moments that you have to go through. In this case, ensure that you make use of the positive vibes that have been with you all along, and spend more time on thinking how the day had made you learn a lot of other things and how you can improve from all the lessons learnt.

4.4 Put Yourself in Practice

In life, if you expect someone else to make things happen for you, that is one of the biggest mistakes that you will ever make. You should be in charge, and what better way to take charge other than taking charge of your mind.

Determine where you are in life now, and ask yourself where you want to be at a certain time. Once you are sure of your goals, do not look back. Just go for them and keep track of your goals to ensure you are on your way to success.

When your clarity meets your conviction and you apply action to the equation, your world will begin to transform before your eyes. Lisa Nichols

4.5 Speaking and Presenting Structure

As mentioned in the earlier paragraphs, it is important for us to have a clear aspiration as it allows us to become more focused in our thoughts and actions.

As a leader, when you speak and present in public, having a clear aspiration is undeniably an essential tool. This is so because when you speak or present, your speech or presentation needs to have a clear purpose and outcome that benefits your audience.

Your speaking and presenting structure should be designed based on your aspiration. For example, at the end of my presentation, I would like my audience to appreciate their life to the fullest. Once you are clear on your aspiration, it is easy for you to plan your presentation. You can then ask yourself questions, such as what stories do you want to share, what examples could enhance the understanding of your audience, what pictures do you want your audience to visualise, what activities do you want your audience to participate in.

A clear aspiration makes a powerful presentation, from the start to the end!

4.5.1 Why You Need to Have a Structured Speaking and Presenting Plan

'She was speaking all over the place! It was hard for the audience to keep track.'

'The presentation was confusing from the very beginning. There was no introduction, and the speaker zoomed into some points before he actually mentioned the objectives of the topic.'

'At the end of the presentation, we were left wondering what the conclusion of his speech was. He didn't do a good job with the closure. It was frustrating.'

Based on the examples above, I believe you can see how important it is for a speaker to have a structured speech or presentation. Beginning with an end in mind is an important concept that applies in every structured presentation.

Before even embarking on any presentation, ask yourself these questions:

- Who is my audience?
- What do I want my audience to receive?
- What do I want my audience to do next?

As you can see, every question revolves around the interest of the audience because a structured presentation ensures that it impacts them significantly. You will be able to stress your points during different parts of your presentation, ensuring that your audience receives the messages that you are delivering and that they are able to effectively use and/or apply what they have received.

A structured presentation will allow you to present with greater confidence as you have an idea of the overall configuration of your speech.

It is also much easier for you to add on your audiovisual aids and vary your speaking style as you are able to see where you are in the presentation.

4.5.2 How to Structure Your Speaking and Presenting

Based on my own experience, I recommend every presentation structure to use a five-stage format which will be further elaborated below.

- **The Five-Stage Format**

A structured presentation should consist of five different parts to it, namely the pre-introduction, introduction, main body, summary, and conclusion.

Stage 1 – Pre-Introduction

It is best to have a pre-introduction before you start your actual introduction to the audience. This is to allow certain variations to occur before you start presenting.

However, do not go overboard with pre-introductions because an effective one will just involve saying casual things which serve no other purpose than to capturing the attention of the audience. No heavy talk at this time, please!

Pre-introductions give space for the audience to start paying attention to you so that you can be sure that by the time you start with your introduction, the audience is all ears.

As a matter of fact, it is also a good head start for you as a speaker to settle into your own pace. The first few seconds (or minutes) in front of your audience can be slightly overwhelming, and a pre-introduction can certainly calm your nerves down.

A good example to start your pre-introduction is by sharing a brief story that is relevant to your presentation. This moment is important for you as it is the best time to attract the attention of your audience.

Stage 2 – Introduction

The introduction stage may at times be taken lightly by some speakers, but bear in mind that it can be the most important part of your speech, and if done right, you will be able to capture your audience's attention throughout your entire speech.

The beginning of your speech gives your audience their first impression not only of your topic and purpose of you sharing the topic, but it will also give them a chance to evaluate you. Therefore, you need to catch their interest from a very, very early point in your speech.

At this stage, I would recommend for you to provide an overview of your presentation, namely, what are the objectives, what are the topics that you will talk about, what are your expectations and the expectations of your audience.

Stage 3 – Main Body

At this stage, you will be presenting your audience with a set of key points which have been effectively organised and supported by the necessary verbal and audiovisual aids.

Your main points need to be simple and straightforward for them to be easily remembered and understood. This is why they should be backed by examples, illustrations, and clarifications.

Stage 4 – Summary

The point of having a summary is to ensure that the audience gets the main points that you have delivered during the main body stage of your presentation.

Summaries encapsulate the keywords of your main points, and they need to be concise and to the point.

Stage 5 – Conclusion

A common mistake made by some speakers is that they did not have a proper closure to their speech. When this happens, the audience is left feeling perplexed and at a loss because they do not know what to expect next.

An effective conclusion is as important as all the other stages as it brings the audience back to an overall understanding of your entire presentation, and reinforce of what you want your audience to do next.

At some point of your speech, some members of the audience may have missed or forgotten a fact, misunderstood or even failed to understand some of the messages that you have delivered. Therefore, a good conclusion will address the issues faced by these audience members.

4.5.3 What You Need to Do to Keep Your Structure in Order

Regardless of your audience, you should always aim to give a structured delivery. Notwithstanding this, how do you ensure that your structure is in order? How do you know exactly what to say and when you should say it?

As I have mentioned earlier, the clarity of your aspiration is a crucial element to assist you in getting your thoughts and actions in order. With clarity, you will be able to establish your thoughts and systematically organise them before putting everything into action.

Ask yourself, "Have you achieved your aspiration?" and "Has your audience achieved their aspiration?"

4.6 Put Yourself in Practice

It is important to note that the best presentations are well-structured ones containing ideas that connect with one another and stories that flow and transition smoothly.

Practise structuring your thoughts as it is an effective way of ensuring that the translation of these thoughts into your presentation allow listeners to keep track of your main points without getting confused and disoriented along the way.

4.7 Well-Designed Preparation

A well-designed preparation is as important as your presentation to the audience. Imagine how disorganised and uncoordinated you will be if you are not adequately prepared. It will certainly impact your audience in an undesirable manner.

4.8 Why You Need a Well-Designed Preparation

'I don't think he made any research before presenting to us because the content was not relevant to what we were interested in.'

'The speaker made numerous mistakes from the very beginning right up to the end of her presentation. Every time she made a mistake, she became more nervous!'

'It was a boring presentation. He was very long-winded, and on top of that, the content was a bit too detailed.'

'He came totally unprepared for the presentation. If he does this again, he will surely not be invited to speak again.'

These are all examples of what can happen to you if you speak without a well-designed preparation.

4.8.1 Meet Your Audience's Expectations

When you craft your presentation, it should all be about meeting the needs and expectations of your audience. Find out who they are and what they are hoping to receive or achieve out of your presentation.

There is no point in being fancy with your content or sharing up-to-date information when it is something that your audience has no interest in.

If you want to keep their attention and focus on you, your presentation should be tailored to the audience accordingly. Spend time researching on their preferences so that you can impress them with the data that they are looking for.

Wouldn't it be unfortunate to have fantastic content but something that the audience does not appreciate at all?

4.8.2 Increase Your Self-Confidence

Well-designed preparations will undeniably intensify your confidence level, which will make your delivery smoother, steadier, and more consistent.

It will also avoid you from making too many mistakes, such as forgetting what to say or experiencing awkward pauses because you cannot find the right word to say next.

With necessary preparation, you will feel positive and energised to speak and share your content with the audience.

4.8.3 Organised and Structured Content

Having a well-designed preparation allows you to produce interesting and remarkable content that is organised and structured in a manner that is easy for you to convey to the audience. Similarly, the audience will not feel pressured to receive them from you as opposed to having too much (or even nothing much)!

Preparations will let you have an avenue to see whether you are able to present with clarity so that your audience knows what you are trying to tell them. In the course of your preparation, you can arrange and rearrange your content, your presentation style, and your presentation tools to ensure that they will be just right for your audience.

Preparing for the content will give you the opportunity to gain prior feedback from your family, friends, colleagues, coach, or mentor as this is a useful way to get honest responses, which can help you improve your presentation.

For example, you may think that your content and the way you have presented it is awesome; however, it might be completely boring for your audience. Rehearsing it first is, therefore, a great idea to ensure that you have some idea on how to give the best presentation to your audience on the day of the event. That way, you can work on the flow of the content and make sure that the presentation is a lively one!

4.9 How You Can Have a Well-Designed Preparation

By having a well-designed preparation, you will be able to convey your message to the audience with clarity and certainty, and they will certainly keep their focus on you, specifically on the content of your speech. But how do you have a well-designed preparation?

A well-designed presentation means that you have undergone a brainstorming session/s to get ideas before selecting the best ideas and, thereafter, connecting and organising them in such a manner that it produced a spectacular content for your audience. You will also have to prepare your necessary audiovisual aids that can support your content and turn your presentation into an impressive and exciting one.

All these will be explained further below.

But before that, take note of these important elements:

4.9.1 Get the Right Topic

Getting the right topic of your presentation is very essential. In some cases, speakers will be given specific topics to speak on; however, there are also times where you are required to come up with your own topic.

In the latter instance, how do you start with choosing the right topic? Do you go for something that you already know a lot about or something that you feel is interesting and will benefit the audience?

Choosing a topic that you are very familiar with will certainly make you feel more confident. There is nothing wrong in this so long as the topic is something that the audience will be interested in.

Choosing a topic that the audience will be fascinated in is a great idea; however, you have to ensure that you are good in it so that you are able to make your audience understand the topic better. It is not enough that they are interested in it but do not have any understanding about it because of your poor delivery.

Do not select topics that you are not interested in as it will be hard to interest your audience if you yourself do not have any interest in it.

4.9.2 Outline Your Speech – Yes, It's Petty but Very Useful!

When you have a speech outline, it means that you have a detailed account of all the critical parts of your speech, which comprise of, amongst others, the topic's title, purpose, objectives, introduction, main points, closing, transitions, and visual aids.

Having an outline helps you organise your ideas better as you are then able to see a general idea of your speech. It makes it a lot simpler to have subtopics from your main topic, according to their significance.

Outlining your speech will also make it much easier for you to identify any issues at an earlier stage of your speech drafting. Furthermore, you will not be tempted to memorise your speech as you have a solid outline to work from, and this gives you flexibility when presenting to your audience.

- **Brainstorm**

In a well-designed preparation, brainstorming is the first step that you take. It is a creative process. This is the phase where a lot of ideas are involved—good or bad. The best part of a brainstorming session is that you can let your mind wander to various ideas and possibilities. There is no limit to it, of course, but at the end of this exercise, you must be able to set aside the nonexceptional ones.

Brainstorming processes can be done on your own, or you can also do it with a group of selected people. If you choose the latter, do include people from various industries and backgrounds to get a good mix of ideas. One small idea can evolve into a really interesting concept, so do not worry if your brainstorming group gets a little bit overenthusiastic with their ideas!

Some people brainstorm by writing on whiteboards, drawing, doodling, taking notes using their smart phones, or even scribbling down on small pieces of paper. Whichever way works for you, go with it because brainstorming is supposed to be a process that is most comfortable to you to get the creative juices flowing.

- **Connect Your Ideas**

Once you have all the ideas you can get out of your brainstorming session/s, it is now time to connect them. Ideas should be interconnected from one point to the next to have a proper flow of content.

Let us assume you managed to obtain three great ideas out of your brainstorming session with a group of friends. The ideas are fantastic on their own; however, you cannot seem to relate them to one another.

If this happens, it means that there is no connectivity amongst the ideas, and you run the risk of getting your audience confused.

- **Organise Your Ideas**

Once your ideas are connected to one another, organise them in such a manner that it makes a presentation smooth, straightforward, and easy to understand.

What you need to ensure is to move smoothly from one point to the other between the different stages of your presentation. It is advisable to use transitions, i.e., certain phrases to avoid any disconnect, for example: *'I'll be sharing three points with you, and I'll first start with (*point 1*) before moving on to (*point 2*) and (*point 3*).'*

By mentioning this to your audience, you are giving them an outline of what they should be expecting from your presentation.

Based on the example above, once you have presented **point 1**, you may say the following: *'In the same way with *point 1*, *point 2* also covers...'*

This ensures that the audience are keeping track with your presentation and that they are informed of what they have been presented with, what they will be presented next, and how the ideas are interconnected with one another.

Then again, it is entirely up to you how you use the necessary transitions between your points so long as there is no broken link.

Randomly jumping into points can mean that you are disorganised or even seen to be trying to avoid elaborating on certain points.

- **Prepare Your Audiovisual Aids**

In this day and age, audiovisual aids are regarded as effective tools to facilitate presentations as they can reinforce or further clarify your main points. They can be anything that supplement and enhance your presentation as long as it helps your audience follow your flow of ideas and understand the message you are delivering across.

Examples of common audiovisual aids used by presenters are LCD projectors, computers, and multimedia. PowerPoint presentations have gained popularity amongst speakers as they are used to present animations and simulations, which can convey complex information in a simple and interesting manner. Bear in mind the usage of fonts and colours as using unfitting ones during your presentation can affect your audience's focus and interest.

The audiovisual aids must be relevant to explain certain messages and not just there as fancy display items. You may also consider avoiding too much dramatisation effects on your animations as your audience might get a headache out of having too many of them.

If your audiovisual aids are fully utilised in the manner they are supposed to be, they are able to offer credibility to your presentation, and you will definitely feel more relaxed and confident when presenting your ideas to the audience.

Notwithstanding this, do avoid poor audiovisual aids which will only cause unnecessary distractions. They should be able to effectively trigger and engage your audience's senses instead of making them dazed and confused. Not only do the audience need to listen to you speak, but they need to pay attention to your audiovisual aids at the same time, and it is a lot to take in!

Remember that the audiovisual aids are there to support and emphasise your main points. The audience should benefit from this as they can separate the more important information from the lesser ones and these are the takeaways that they really need.

Be in control of your audiovisual aids, and do not go overboard with them!

4.10 What You Need to Do to Keep Your Preparation Well-Designed

A well-designed preparation means that you have ensured the following:

1. A straightforward content structure which is easy for you to convey your message and easy for your audience to follow.
2. A presentation that is 'easy on the eyes'—make good decisions to use the right font type and size and make good use of colours in your presentation (not too colourful or too monotonous).
3. Summarised key takeaways so that the audience is able to pick out what is really important from the information that you have shared.
4. Share just enough information on the presentation slides—carefully select your words and write and rewrite until you get the right text. Not too wordy, please. Bullet points are fine.
5. Edit and keep editing until your presentation is refined and ready for the audience.

4.11 Put Yourself in Action

As you can see, preparation is essential for the success of your presentation; hence, it is important to spend some time and effort on it. The more you prepare and practise for your presentation, the better it will be.

From the very beginning, identify the purpose of your presentation and ensure that it is extremely clear for you and the audience. Once this is established, it will put less pressure for you to craft your presentation in the manner that you believe your audience will appreciate.

4.12 Put It All Together

Time to put all the pieces together!

At this stage, you already have a proper structure and your content is drafted. The next crucial step is to draw up your presentation based on the research and materials that you have prepared.

4.13 Order of the Speaking and Presentation

In summary, based on what I have explained in the earlier paragraphs, I would like to suggest nine basic steps in preparing the order of your speech/presentation:

1. Select the topic of your speech/presentation.
2. Determine the purpose of your speech/presentation.
3. Determine the objectives of your speech/presentation.
4. Perform an audience analysis.
5. Connect and organise your ideas.
6. Outline your speech/presentation.
7. Prepare a five-stage format of your speech/presentation.
8. Prepare your audiovisual aids effectively.
9. Rehearse your speech/presentation.

4.14 How You Deliver Your Speech and Presentation

Having gone through the basic steps mentioned earlier, it is time to start preparing how to present for each different stage of your speech.

- **How to Start Your Introduction (Facts, Asking Questions, Storytelling)**

In the process of crafting your speech, bear in mind that a good strong introduction is crucial because it can either make or break your entire speech. It is up to your creativity on how you wish to begin your speech.

Some speakers start off by asking questions to the audience to loosen up the interaction process. However, it is best to stick to rhetorical questions to just trigger the minds of the audience, i.e., to get them going. No point asking questions which require them to respond in perfect answers and, in the process, giving them headache and mental stress even at the very beginning of your presentation!

Some others prefer to commence their session with a fact or statistics, and this also works; however, the fact must relate to the topic at hand. You may use facts by renowned and esteemed figures or institutions to immediately capture the interest of your audience.

Another fantastic way to begin your speech is by sharing a personal story. That way, the audience can relate to you better because they may have shared common experiences, challenges, or goals with you. The story can be emotional or humorous so long as it is able to fascinate your audience instead of irking them.

All these methods will depend on how comfortable both you and your audience will feel. The objective is to intrigue your audience and make them want to look forward to listen to the rest of your speech.

During the introduction process, your audience should be made aware of the topic that you are presenting, its purpose and main points. The trick here is to just share an outline of what you will be presenting without giving too much away. That way, your audience will be piqued, and they cannot wait to hear what you have to say as they are already expecting some of the points based on what you have shared.

- **How to Deliver Your Content**

After your introduction, the next stage is to start presenting your main points which are considered the backbone of your speech.

In the process of crafting your speech, ensure that each main point is supported with materials that your audience will find useful; for example, the use of illustrations, interesting stories, anecdotes, or other attention-grabbing information.

Be careful not to overload your audience with too much visual or verbal aids as they might not be able to process the main points that you have delivered.

The main body of your speech should encompass clarifications and pieces of evidence that can be easily understood by the audience. On that note, depending, of course, on your speech content, try not to have too many main points—it is best to stick to a range of three to five main points. Organise your main points well, and your audience will certainly be kept captivated throughout this stage of your presentation.

- **How to Summarise Your Speaking and Presentation**

There are two ways that you can do this.

One way is to summarise the main points after you have finished presenting all the main points during the main body stage.

Another way is to summarise after making each point.

Whichever way works best for you and your audience, do note that summaries should be brief and short. You can be very creative in the manner you summarise and recall your main points as long as the summaries support the message you are trying to get across.

- **How to Conclude Your Speaking and Presentation**

A conclusion is basically a recap of your speech, not an introduction of new information. At this stage, the audience is looking forward to hear a wrap-up, and it is best to keep your conclusion relatively brief. A strategic close can profoundly impact the audience, and this is what you should be aiming for.

A good conclusion includes a summary of your main points and ideas. At this point, you may also like to challenge or to appeal to your audience to act on what you have shared.

You may end with a powerful quotation or phrase so that the powerful or memorable words will linger in their minds and provide them a boost to take their next actions/steps.

- **Put Yourself into Action**

After completing the order of your speech, run through the flow to see whether they are interconnected and/or they make complete sense of what you are trying to convey.

Take time to refine the draft and do not hesitate to review it until you are fully confident to present the final copy to your audience.

4.15 Preparation before Presentation

'I have a feeling the speaker did not rehearse his lines. He looked so unprepared. He was shuffling his notes, looking for things to say. It was frustrating to watch.'

'You wouldn't believe how late she was! When she finally arrived, about a quarter of the audience members had already left because they had important meetings to attend to. The ones who stayed back were already fidgeting in their seats and were not that focused during her presentation as well!'

'The speaker seemed to be a bit lost during his speech. It was as if he was so unfamiliar with the room layout, and it sort of distracted him. I sincerely feel that he should have checked out the place first to get a sense of familiarity.'

'There was a problem with her presentation slides. Apparently, it uses a different software and was not able to be uploaded. She should have checked with the organisers earlier.'

'The opening was quite hilarious. The emcee had introduced the speaker, and she clearly wasn't happy with how she was introduced to the audience. You could see it in her face!'

- **Rehearse, Rehearse, Rehearse**

You may think that you have done several presentations in your life so much that you do not need to rehearse your next presentation. *But do you know that even highly-experienced speakers devote their time to preparing for their presentation, in this case, rehearsing for it?*

Opportunity to Practice

Rehearsing for your presentation allows you to practise as many times as possible within your comfort zone before delivering it in front of an audience. A rehearsal session is a space where you can try out various delivery methods to see which one works best with your audience.

I believe that if you want to deliver an impactful and successful presentation, you will need to spend considerable time preparing for it because the more you plan and prepare, the more comfortable you will be and the more spontaneous you will appear in front of your audience.

Just like feeling bored and frustrated when watching a movie where actors seemed to be reading through their scripts, your audience will feel the same way if your speech is flat and dull because you are merely reading from your notes rather than interacting with them. This is why you need to work your lines, practise your facial expressions and body language, try different speaking styles, etc., to make sure that your presentation will flow naturally.

- **Eliminate Stress and Fear**

Practising consistently will not only boost your confidence up a level (or many levels!), but it will also make you remember your materials and make you more accustomed to it. Think about it: Unfamiliarity with your own content and research materials will crumble your confidence as you feel that you do not own it, hence not in control of your own presentation.

Feeling nervous speaking in front of an audience is one thing, but imagine if you come totally unprepared. Wouldn't that make matters worse for you? Your stress level will increase, and your fear, with regard to presenting your materials in front of your audience, will definitely deepen.

If you have had several rounds rehearsing for it, you will feel much better when facing your crowd; therefore, even if you do feel anxious or worried about speaking in public, at best, you can be sure that you have prepped your best for it.

- **Rehearsal Tips**

Let me share with you several tips that you can use when practising for your next presentation.

It is advisable to memorise your opening and closing remarks and the key points that you wish to get across to your audience.

Memorising your opening sentence is crucial because it makes you develop your confidence. If you have nailed a great opening, you will feel more comfortable and at ease, and the rest of the content will flow in more smoothly.

Meanwhile, memorising your closing remarks is to ensure that you have a solid end to your presentation. Just in case your audience had felt a bit lost within your speech, a good concluding speech will help direct them towards what they are missing.

Memorising your key points is crucial as it serves as a guide when you speak. How you memorise it is entirely up to your preference as long as it makes sense to you and it can trigger your memory of the rest of the content that you have prepared for.

I always feel that practising in front of the mirror works for me because I am able to see my facial expressions and body language when I speak. I can work on toning my presentation based on what I see and hear.

Once you have practised by yourself, do not stop there. Record your rehearsal so that you can reflect on your own presentation. When you view a recording of your rehearsal, put yourself in the shoes of your audience. How do you think you performed? Did you like what you have seen? Or heard? What other improvements do you like to see? Take notes and see how best you can improve your presentation.

When you feel that you are confident with your presentation, get a few family members, close friends, your coach or mentor to sit through your rehearsal. Ask them for their honest opinions, gather their feedback, and work on things that you need to improve on. They may have pointed out flaws which you had not noticed before. It is always good to know about these way ahead of your actual presentation.

As a final tip, do remember that despite the need to rehearse several times, do not rehearse in excess as it will only exhaust you and can even make you lose interest in your own presentation! Rehearse effectively and sufficiently to obtain fantastic results.

- **Arrive Early**

Save all your travel stress and please arrive early on the day of your presentation. For one, you do not want to arrive looking like a nervous wreck, rummaging through bags and files for your notes or speaking points.

Remember that all eyes are already on you the moment you stand in front of your audience, and they will be looking at every single detail that they witness, and they will be quick to conclude on how unprepared you are to speak.

- **Run Your Points**

Arriving early gives you splendid opportunity to run your points quickly in your mind. The advantage is that you are already feeling at ease because time is on your side; therefore, you will not feel rushed whilst you are trying to remember your points.

Arriving late during your presentation will only cause your points to be jumbled in your mind because you are already feeling pressed for time. Instead of appearing cool, calm, and collected in front of your audience, you will only appear to look and sound unprepared and not ready to face them.

- **Connect with the Audience**

One of the best advantages to arrive early is to have the opportunity to mingle with your audience, i.e., the people you are trying to impress and connect with.

It is a good idea to be around at the registration area and build rapport with your audience for you to get to know them better. This is the best time to have a rough idea about their hopes and expectations from your presentation. Not only will this exercise help you work on the tone of your presentation, but it will also give your audience a wonderful opportunity to connect and be comfortable with you.

- **Listen to Other Speakers**

If you are speaking in a conference where there are other speakers apart from you, it is advisable to arrive early so that you have an opportunity to listen to the other speakers.

It may be too late for you to adjust your presentation so that it is 'better' than the other speakers'; however, there is always an opportunity to improve your style and tone of presentation as you have a brief idea on what works/does not work with the audience based on their reaction towards other speakers.

However, do not get overwhelmed by the other speakers, so much so that you lose your confidence to speak!

4.15.1 Check the Layout of Room or Venue

Before your presentation, it is a good idea to get to the room or venue early because it will give you ample time to settle in and adapt to your physical presentation space.

It is best to do a site visit because the sense of familiarity will help you during your presentation.

If this is not practical, ask the organisers for a layout of the venue and/or some photos of the venue so you have an idea of how the place looks like before you speak at the actual event day to get a sense of the physical space.

It may just be a venue, but it can influence your performance as a speaker and can also indirectly impact the audience. Therefore, you should scope the venue and ensure that you are comfortable with the seating arrangement, audiovisual aids, room temperature, or any possible noise or distractions that can affect your presentation.

By familiarising yourself with the venue location and settings, your mind will be at ease, and you will feel more comfortable to speak. These may seem like trifling issues to consider; however, they can really make a difference to your performance.

4.15.2 Check that Everything Works and That You Can Work Everything

Let us not assume that everything will work out fine during the day just because there have never been any technical glitches in your past presentations.

You may have rehearsed your presentation several times; however, like all 'live' events, something can happen the way you did not intend it to.

This is why it is best to always check for anything and everything related to your presentation before you start presenting. Find out in advance who are the technicians, floor managers, or people in charge for your event and ensure that you and all of them are on the same page regarding your presentation expectations (in terms of the technical aspects specifically).

Always test your microphones and PowerPoint slides to see that they are working correctly. Do you need handheld or lapel microphones? Do you need help from the organiser to click through your presentation? All these must be looked into and resolved way before you start speaking to audience. You do not want to be seen as the speaker who is struggling on stage because of technical issues that could have been addressed earlier.

Similarly, if you need help with the lighting and sound system, you will need to put in your request to the people in charge, and you should not assume that everything is a done deal. It will be stressful for you as a speaker and very uncomfortable for the audience to watch if glitches like this appear before or whilst you are speaking to them.

Every speaker requires different needs, and it is up to you as a speaker to put in any specific request.

4.15.3 Check How You Will Be Introduced

Do you know how important your introduction is? Extremely!

However, more often than not, introductions are overlooked and taken casually by speakers.

It is best to provide the emcee with a draft on how you wish to be introduced to the audience. The introduction should address your credentials; for example your academic qualifications, working and life experiences, awards, and other accomplishments.

Stick to information which you feel will be of relevance and interest to the audience. Do not prepare an essay for it as it can only bore your audience and make them lose interest in what you have to present! Less is more, but ensure what you share is of significance to your audience and that it is something that will boost their trust and interest in you.

4.15.4 Put Yourself into Action

There are many other small things that you can tick off your checklist as preparation before your presentation.

Some of these include checking where the restrooms, prayer rooms, and refreshment areas are. Believe it or not, if you have unknown factors in the back of your mind, it can put you in an uneasy state.

Finally, even after thorough preparation, you have to admit the fact that not everything will be perfect (or almost perfect) or run smoothly at the event.

Notwithstanding this, you know that you have prepared well and that you were mentally and physically ready to speak to your audience. And because of this, you deserve a pat in the back!

CHAPTER 5

Behaviour

5.1 Introduction

As a presenter and speaker, the last thing you want to do is create a negative impression about yourself. However, speakers sometimes forget the basic necessities of public speaking: appearance and personality. Because of this unnecessary blunder, they often lose out on a number of things, primarily, in convincing their audience with what they have to say.

5.2 High-Impact Presentation of Yourself

Having high-impact presentation skills ensures the ability of the speaker to adapt to speaking in public in front of various types of audience. Not only will the speaker be able to acclimatise to the surroundings, but the speaker will also be able to effectively deliver remarkable speeches and presentations.

5.2.1 Why You Need to Have a High-Impact Self-Presentation

High-impact self-presentation is a skill that will give you that added boost because you will appear confident, convincing, and inspiring to your audience. You will be able to engage and connect with them at a level that meets or even surpasses their expectations of you.

Your audience will be hooked on your speech and presentation, and essentially, they will like you. When an audience likes a speaker, they put their trust on the speaker, and they will keep their minds open, which, consequently, is a plus point for speakers to relay their message across effectively.

5.2.2 How to Ensure You Have a High-Impact Self-Presentation

Our appearance and personality are significant factors in determining if we have a high-impact self-presentation.

- **Appearance**

'He looked like he had just woken up five minutes ago! His hair was dishevelled, and he looked extremely groggy!'

'It was a formal function, but I was surprised that the speaker came in with an untucked shirt. He even had the first three buttons of his shirt off, and it was quite an awkward scene for the audience.'

'Her nails were dirty. I couldn't focus on anything else!'

'She had heavy makeup on, and I was afraid that her false eyelashes would fall off! We were also distracted by the excessive amount of jewellery she had on her.'

These are all examples of feedback received from audience members who undoubtedly were preoccupied by their speaker's appearance instead of the speech made.

To look the part of the message that you want to put across to your audience, how you dress is important. In addition to your overall attitude, appearance plays an important role in public speaking as it reflects your seriousness towards the message that you are conveying.

Do consider the following important guidelines when it comes to appearance:

- **Clothing**

Always wear appropriate and comfortable clothing when speaking or presenting to your audience. You might be a fan of loud, gaudy, or even multiple-coloured clothing, but during formal speeches and presentations, these should be avoided. You want your audience to regard you as a person of authority and not having them picture you as a clown from their childhood!

Notwithstanding this, if you choose colours that are excessively monotonous, you might end up being pictured as part of the wall, hence making your presence completely forgettable. Shoes must be polished and clothes must be ironed and kept tidy because you do not want the audience to regard you as a lazy speaker who cares less about looking good for them, what more to give them an impactful speech.

Tip: Wear clothing that echoes what you have to say, not clothing that dominates the show.

- **Accessories and Makeup**

Accessories and makeup should be kept to a minimum. Too much 'bling' and/or heavy cosmetics will distract your audience's attention from the content of your speech. Bear in mind that it is not your intention to attract them to your watches and jewelleries or to the colour of your eye shadow, rouge, or lip gloss. Rather, it is the content of your speech that the audience should place their focus on. The idea is to look presentable instead of attracting your audience for all the wrong reasons.

Tip: Wear minimum accessories and makeup, with least possible impact.

- **Hygiene and Health**

Speakers with poor hygiene are often regarded as unhealthy and unkempt. To avoid being perceived this way, you need to maintain good personal grooming to create a great impression amongst your audience. These include ensuring that your hair is neatly combed, that your fingernails are clean, and that you do not have any bad breath or body odour. High-impact speaking requires a great deal of confidence, and the more confidence you have, the more impactful and effective you will be in relaying your message across. Healthy living and engaging in some form of regular physical activity is good for both physical and mental preparation for speaking in front of your audience.

Tip: Personal grooming and healthy living are essential. Do not skip the process.

- **Personality**

'I came by to tell her how excited I was to listen to her speak, but she didn't even bat an eyelid. I was just an audience member, so I guess I wasn't important to her. Because of her reaction, I lost interest and couldn't focus during her speech.'

'I didn't dare pose a question during the Q&A session after I saw how he had ridiculed an audience member for asking a valid question. His action was uncalled for!'

'I won't be attending any more of his speech presentations in the future. It was pretty exhausting to see how unyielding he was. A bit narrow-minded for a professional like him to take a rigid stand!'

'We wanted to hear more examples of what he had to say, but he seemed a bit selfish in his sharing. It was hard for us to relate, and at the end of the session, we didn't grasp as much information as we had wanted. Quite a waste of time, really.'

The above are some examples of what a speaker's nightmare sounds like! In each example, you can see how frustrated, disappointed, and upset the audience members felt—before, during, or after a speaker's speech.

Different speakers have different styles when making a speech, and this style will or will not make a speech memorable to the audience. The speaker's personality will also be infused in the speech, intentionally or otherwise. The good news is if the speaker has a fantastic personality, the probability of his speech being as fantastic is high, of course, subject to the speech content. Nonetheless, if the speaker's personality is a far cry from superb, his speech might not be as impactful as he would have wanted, even if he has delivered great content!

Therefore, it is important to consider your own personality and evaluate how you naturally interact with others. You may be friendly and approachable when you speak with friends in a coffee house, but you might not carry the same personality when you speak in front of an audience in a formal setting. You may also have the same dull and dreary personality which you carry everywhere you go!

As a speaker, you have to remember that your audience is there to listen to you speak and present your views, ideas, or recommendations. They have allocated time to be there, to open their minds and to put their trust in you as an expert in what you are conveying to them.

It is only fair that you grant them a favour in return by presenting yourself as a speaker with a pleasant and good-natured personality.

The following are some excellent personality traits of a highly-impactful speaker:

- **Respectful and Polite**

Some speakers have been known to be rude to the audience members because of the words and gestures they use, for example, laughing or making fun of an audience member's question because it was 'silly' or 'trivial' to the speaker. It is never a good idea to belittle your audience. Your being there as a speaker is to educate and enlighten them about a particular topic, and your speech will not be considered effective or impactful if your audience does not favour your personality in the process of you conveying the topic to them.

Tip: Do not offend.

- **Approachable**

Your personality kicks not only during or after your speech, but also even before your speech starts. For example, it is only normal for audience members to come up to you prior to your speech for various reasons, perhaps just to say hello. Regardless of the reason, as a speaker, you should maintain to be approachable. Nevertheless, if you sincerely believe that they are either distracting your focus before you speak, or asking questions prematurely, you can politely decline to answer or excuse yourself without having to appear disrespectful. By doing this, you will indirectly gain the respect of the respective audience members, and they will not feel disappointed or lose interest in your upcoming speech.

Tip: Become someone who is easy to talk to.

- **Open-Minded and Sharing**

Some speakers have the view that they are all-knowing and mistake-free presenters, so much so that they are rigid in their thoughts and opinions. Speakers with this personality type are regarded by the audience as selfish. This egotistical behaviour is something that you should entirely avoid as the audience would label you as someone who is too opinionated and prejudiced in your views. The entire presentation will then be a one-way interaction with the audience feeling disgusted with your behaviour.

Tip: Speak with an open mind and learn to share for the benefit of others.

- **What You Need to Practise to Keep a High-Impact Self-Presentation**

Apart from maintaining a good appearance and personality, you can add in the following essentials to ensure that you convey a highly-impactful speech to your audience.

- **Voice**

Your voice plays an important role in your speech performance. Some speakers are gifted with having just the right speaking voice, i.e., one that has strength and authority and that can attract the attention of the audience.

Alas, not all speakers have the right tone of voice to have a bearing on their audience. You might have a squeaky, high-pitched voice, or a voice that is too loud or booming, or a type of voice that could make your audience's positive impression of you go down the drain.

If you want to communicate effectively and ensure that your speech can impact your audience, you must practise the pitch, tone, and volume of your voice. That way, you can present your message and emphasise on certain points much better. However, be careful with your vocal variety. If you maintain a loud tone of voice and high volume, your audience might regard you as someone who is overly aggressive; on the other hand, if you speak using a soft tone and low volume, you might come across as someone who is too timid.

- **Drama**

Dramatising a speech is a smart way of capturing your audience's attention; nevertheless, be wary of the extent of adding variety to your speech. To help you emphasise a certain message to your audience, you can have a moment of silence or a dramatic pause in your sentence. Dropping a little suspense in your speech is fine; however, it is not advisable to go overboard as your audience might get 'lost' in your presentation, and they might not be able to grasp what you really want to convey to them.

5.3 Put Yourself in Action

At the end of the day, when making a speech, you have to be calm, focused, and in control of your behaviour. You only have a limited time with your audience, and during that moment, you have to make them feel comfortable with you, you have to convince them, and you have to keep them interested. It is not a tall order if you truly enjoy the session and likewise for your audience.

5.4 How You Deliver Your Message

We have spoken about how your appearance and personality play key roles in ensuring that you have a highly-impactful self-presentation. We will now look at an important aspect that you need to manage when delivering your message across to your audience.

As a speaker, your effectiveness is determined via your ability to attract your audience's attention, interest, and emotion not only through verbal but also nonverbal communication. This is because your audience judge you and the message you are conveying based on what they hear and what they see. Therefore, in addition to your voice and vocal variety, your body language and gestures are also significant elements that you can use to communicate a highly-impactful speech.

5.5 High-Impact Body Language

Whether we realise it or not, from a very young age, we have begun to express ourselves using our body language. For example, when we were little, we pout to express our disappointment or anger over something. It is how we learn to have our needs met.

As we grow older, we start using a series of body language signals, which are more refined, to ensure that the people we are communicating with are able to pick up the signals without us having to say anything to them.

There are various types of body language. Whilst some types are easy for people to read, some others are not. Amongst the forms of body language are romantic, greeting, aggressive, attentive, bored, closed, deceptive, defensive, dominant, emotional, evaluating, open, powerful, ready, relaxed, and submissive.

5.5.1 Why You Need to Have a High-Impact Body Language

Your body language can send 'hidden messages' to your audience. Believe it or not, every part of your body is used in body language, and whether you intend to make each movement or not, or whether there is a presence or absence of movement, these can all mean something to other people who are observing you.

Body language combines movements, gestures, and postures, including how a speaker talks, moves, and looks on stage. Therefore, body language is significant as it forms part of the message that a speaker wants to give.

Having a high-impact body language will strengthen your position on stage, and it shows your high confidence level to the audience. Your audience starts observing you within seconds of you being in front of them, and if your body language exerts negative vibes, they will not trust you, which, ultimately, will decrease your chances of capturing their attention and interest with your speech. *Keep in mind that your body language can make or break your presentation because your movements, gestures, and postures exude an important message.*

5.5.2 How to Perform a High-Impact Body Language

'I had a bit of an awkward experience today. The speaker gave me too much eye contact. Made me feel uneasy throughout his presentation.'

'She seems to have a habit of biting her fingernails whenever an audience member asks a question. I think she's nervous!'

'It would be good to see his face when he speaks. Most of the time, he turns his back to us or he sits behind the lectern.'

'We noticed that his face seemed a bit tight throughout his speech. Not sure what was making him angry. The frown obviously showed!'

The above are some examples of bad body language. You, as a speaker, would not have noticed it, but to the audience, your body language is obviously sending them adverse messages.

Every individual is different, and not everyone exhibits the exact same body language when they need to express something. Whilst some speakers use minimal emphasis with their body language, some others tend to overstate the same gesture. Good speakers should manage their body language to ensure that they do not send the wrong signals to their audience.

5.5.3 What You Need to Practise to Keep a High-Impact Body Language

Using your body language effectively and wisely can help you deliver your message with success. Control your body movements and use them with relevance to the message that you are conveying to your audience. Some gestures need only be used sparingly; therefore, do not overdo them. For example, looking at your watch or mobile phone might indicate boredom and that you cannot wait to leave the event!

- **Eye Contact**

Have you ever seen a speaker who avoids the eyes of the audience or his eyes keeps darting around the room? What signal does this send you? In usual cases, a speaker who does this will come across as being insincere or dishonest, despite the fact that the actions were unintentional, as he was feeling nervous or shy to face his audience.

In my earlier years of public speaking, I experienced the same problem too. I had poor eye contact due to my nerves; however, over time, I regarded my audience as a group of people whom I am having sincere conversations with instead of viewing them as a crowd. Doing this helped calm my nerves. I was able to maintain eye contact, and the trick is to only linger for a few seconds on one or a few audience members before randomly maintaining eye contact with another individual or group of people.

You will find that focusing your sight on certain members of the audience will create a bond with them as you make them feel involved and connected to you. Then again, be very careful not to 'cross the line' and maintain too much eye contact with a selected few from your audience as you might create unnecessary awkwardness.

- **Gestures**

You would not want your audience to get distracted by certain gestures that you do when speaking to them whether you realise it or not. What gestures am I referring to here? There are several, of course; for example, fidgeting, nail-biting, lip-biting, or twitching and also other gestures like jingling your keys in your pockets, hiding your hands in your pockets, or scratching your head (when you don't even feel any itch!).

I have also been to conferences where there were speakers who stand on stage with their arms across their chest during Q&A sessions. Naturally, the impression from the audience in cases like this is that the speakers do not wish to welcome feedback or questions from the floor.

All these gestures can distract your audience from focusing on your speech and the key messages that you are trying to convey to them. However hard you try to speak effectively and with high impact, the only thing that your audience sees is how nervous you are via your gestures. When they observe this, the amount of trust they have in you will fade away.

- **Body Positions**

As a speaker, you need to move your body naturally from one spot to another. The best way to do this is to walk to another spot whenever you move to a new point in your speech and move forward, towards the audience, when you are expecting a response from them. Body positions can be subtle but very powerful in conveying messages to the audience. Furthermore, the audience will not have a sense of boredom as you are spreading a form of energy to the room via your movements.

However, as with all cases, do not overdo your movements. Imagine a speaker constantly moving about the stage without any pause or gaps in between. I would expect the audience to feel a bit dizzy after his speech, and what is worse is that they would not gain anything from the speech as they have been too disturbed by his endless movements!

- **Facial Expressions**

You may feel nervous or shy or upset over a certain feedback made by a member of the audience, and your facial expressions will clearly show if you are unable to control it.

Facial expressions are significant in public speaking because the way you look expresses your feelings and your message. Smiling is the best way to express yourself to your audience as it indirectly makes them feel relaxed and comfortable with you. Notwithstanding this, it is not a good idea to be smiling throughout your speech as your facial expressions should be in line with the message that you are conveying.

Practise a variety of facial expressions to emphasise different sections of your speech to pique the interest of your audience.

5.6 Put Yourself into Action

Having high-impact body language simply means that you are focusing on several fundamentals, such as movements, gestures, and postures. Always remember that your body language should not be too much or too little. How do you achieve this? It is not difficult if you constantly practise to get the right balance.

Let me give you a few more examples.

You know you need to maintain eye contact, but it should be just firm enough to convince your audience that their presence is important to you.

You know you need to move your hands to emphasise on certain points, but it should just be enough to ensure that there is no overuse of hands, which could indicate your nervousness.

You know that you need to have a solid posture, so you walk tall because you are confident, but it should not make you look too proud as this could cause your audience to loathe you.

Therefore, be in control. Manage your movements, gestures, and postures so that your audience will be captivated by your speech and not drive them away.

5.7 Speak with Conviction

5.7.1 What Is 'Speak with Conviction'?

'So, uh . . . today my topic is about, uh . . . how to speak confidently, you know, um, speaking with confidence, um . . .'

"Ladies and gentlemen, sorry if this is too much information . . . so sorry . . ."

"Right, uh . . . so let us continue with . . . um . . . okay, let us continue . . . maybe?"

If you want to know what speaking with conviction is, it is definitely not like the above examples at all!

We are usually drawn towards people who speak with confidence. Therefore, when speakers insert word fillers, such as *uh, um, okay, right, so,* and *you know,* in their sentences, they seem to portray the fact that they are not ready to speak. This will indirectly create doubts and uncertainties in the minds of the audience, and they eventually start to lose interest in the speech or presentation.

Overusing the word *sorry* is also a common mistake that speakers make. Instead of gaining the sympathy of the audience by continuously apologising in various points during the speech, this could sometimes backfire.

If we are uncomfortable with our speech, our audience will also feel uncomfortable. Likewise, if we are relaxed and confident, there will be a positive reaction from our audience.

5.7.2 Why You Need to Speak with Conviction

If you are unable to communicate effectively, you will not be able to achieve what you have aimed for. For your message to reach your audience, your style of communication must be assertive and strong. Your expertise, your views, and even the content of your speech or presentation could be excellent, but you have to master how to speak with conviction and confidence.

Speaking with conviction simply means that you are able to convince your audience, make them trust you and believe in what you are delivering to them. You must be willing to do this because if you speak half-heartedly, with flat and dreary tones, the response from the audience will be equally lukewarm.

5.7.3 How to Speak with Conviction

Whilst some speakers are gifted with strong, commanding voices that will turn heads and make people want to listen, others might not be as lucky. To have a commanding voice, you should speak from your diaphragm and practise deepening your voice. Speaking with a deep voice is undoubtedly a better preference in comparison with speaking nasally or in a high-pitched manner.

You may also get a little bit too excited to share your content with the audience, which, in turn, makes you speak too quickly. You have to learn how to speak slowly but not too slow, of course, as your audience will nod themselves to sleep any minute! Speaking slowly with a steady pace allows your audience to capture the essence of your speech without being distracted by the speed of your presentation.

Speaking with conviction is also how very confident you sound in your spoken messages. Speak enthusiastically, with passion, energy, and intensity, and believe me, your audience will get a long-lasting and positive impact once your speech is over.

And remember this, the next time you have the urge of using the *uh* and *um*s in your speech, insert a pause instead to create a more dramatic impact in your presentation. That way, you can also avoid saying things that are irrelevant or annoying to your audience!

- **Listen with Empathy**

What is 'listening with empathy'? Ask yourself these questions: When you listen to others, are you truly hearing them with an open mind? Are you really understanding the person who is talking to you? In essence, are you listening with or without empathy? Empathetic listening is about really going in deep into the nonjudgemental zone. It refers to an emotional connection with others through feeling and understanding. When you have this ability in your communication with other people, you are able to listen with a sincere understanding of their views and ideas without having to judge them.

- **Why You Need to Listen with Empathy**

Take time out to reflect on your family, friends, and acquaintances. You may find that some of them are naturally-born empaths. Have you noticed that when you are in a conversation with this category of people, you feel totally at ease, you are able to relate even your deepest feelings and secrets to them, and you do not feel concerned that they will judge you after all that you have shared with them?

Now I believe you have also crossed paths with a different set of people who makes you feel otherwise. But first, let us not judge those without the skills of empathic listening.

In reality, it is not easy to process the emotions of others, let alone having to deal with them. However, the good news is that empathy skills can be acquired and further developed. More importantly, you need to be willing to keep an open mind and to stay focused within a completely-positive zone. Be patient, and your skills will soon sharpen, especially with practice and repetition.

It is always a good feeling to talk to someone who understands, and by listening with empathy, you will be able to make others feel just that. As human beings, it is normal for us to desire to feel listened to and understood, and when we believe that we are not being heard, we become frustrated, sad, and depressed.

> *There's a power in allowing yourself to be known and heard, in owning your unique story, in using your authentic voice. And there's a grace in being willing to know and hear others. This, for me, is how we become.*
> —Michelle Obama

Then again, bear in mind that being empathetic does not mean agreeing with everything the other person says. It is more of a sincere attempt to understand what others say from their perspectives.

- **How to Listen with Empathy**

You tell yourself that you want to be an empathic listener because it is the best way to reach out and connect with the person you are talking to. But in practice, how do you actually do it?

Let us put ourselves in the shoes of somebody who wishes to communicate our views and opinions to another person. We would surely want to feel comfortable not only with the person we are talking to, but also in the environment around us. Disruptions always make others feel uncomfortable, and they may have a sense that they are not being heard. Avoid potential disruptions, such as ringing phones or other annoying sounds.

Therefore, before anything else, the environment must be a pleasant and comfortable one. This way, both you, as the person listening, and the person you are listening to will have a comfortable zone where you are able to focus on what the person has to say, and likewise, the person is able to express his/her views with ease and assurance. Once a good rapport is established, mutual trust and respect will increase accordingly.

When you speak, you must not 'lose your audience.' What I mean by this is that you should at all times observe their body language and gestures to ensure that they are still listening to your speech or presentation. In your interaction with them, feel free to ask open-ended questions to invite them to share their thoughts on a slightly deeper level, such as "Would you have acted differently, and if yes, why?"

Another important point about listening with empathy is to allow the other party to speak without being interrupted. This skill needs to be mastered because it might not be an easy task in reality.

5.8 Put Yourself in Action

Listening with empathy is critical as it is about understanding how a person feels about something or how a person views a particular issue. In situations like this, trust is built and maintained, and tensions are reduced.

It is a powerful skill to have and one that will be crucial for you as a speaker to use when communicating with your audience.

5.9 How to Overcome Stage Fear

'My heart was beating so fast, I thought I was about to have a heart attack!'

'As soon as I stood in front of everyone, I lost my voice. I just froze, and I couldn't speak at all.'

'My hands were extremely cold and shaky. Even my knees were shaky too!'

'Every time I get called by my boss to present in front of the management team, my mouth starts to dry up, and I feel giddy and nauseated at the same time. I hate the feeling.'

'I bite my nails before and even during speaking. It's embarrassing.'

'My lips tremble when I speak. When I do speak, I'll speak too fast and can't even catch my breath.'

These are only some of the physical symptoms of people who experience stage fright. You might be able to relate to at least one of them. These feelings—coupled with negative thoughts that you are (a) embarrassed to become the centre of attention, (b) worried in your lack of ability to speak in public, or (c) afraid of forgetting what to say to the audience—will, more often than not, cause your performance to fail.

Although public speaking could be your great source of anxiety, it does not mean that the feeling should last forever. Some famous speakers and orators that you know today may have had histories of fears and anxieties themselves when it comes to speaking in public, but they overcame their fears. Through consistent practice and a positive attitude, everyone, including you, can become excellent in public speaking.

In overcoming the fear of public speaking, one of the most common advice that you may hear is to 'let go of any form of stress.' But both you and I know that this is easier said than done. This approach might not work well for everyone. Even telling yourself that you should let go of your stress could lead to more feelings of anxiousness.

Instead, what you should do is to manage the stress. The human body requires some stress for it to function properly; therefore, we need to accept the fact that stress does exist, and what we can do is to manage it well to ensure that it does not overwhelm us.

Think of stress as a form of nervous energy, where you are in an anxious state, such as feeling edgy or uncomfortable. When you are in this state, you will get emotionally imbalanced. What you then need to work on is to manage the stress level so that you have good control over your emotional responses. It is only natural for someone to have nervous energy, but when you are able to harness the energy source to your benefit, you can easily take charge of your emotions and, ultimately, turn your performance into a much better one.

For example, you can use the excess energy within you to make your delivery more dramatic because you can focus on your speech vocalisation and volume. You can also utilise the power of pauses between words to ensure that you make an impactful speech.

Stress serves a purpose. Learning how to harness it, albeit not simple, is doable, and with constant practice, you will be able to use the stress within you as a valuable tool for effective delivery.

I learned that courage was not the absence of fear, but the triumph over it. I felt fear myself more times than I can remember, but I hid it behind a mask of boldness. The brave man is not he who does not feel afraid, but he who conquers that fear. —Nelson Mandela, Long Walk to Freedom, *1994*

5.9.1 Tips

Every speaker manages their fears and anxieties differently. The more speeches and presentations you give, the more it will enable you to learn which strategies and tips work best for you. Here are some which I believe are the most effective:

- **Be Well-Prepared**

Not preparing beforehand is a bad idea as it will make you feel more anxious than ever. Trust me, knowing that you have prepared yourself will lessen your apprehension.

- **Warm Up**

Just like singers who warm up their voices before singing, or athletes who warm up their muscles before their sports activities, as a public speaker, you too need to warm up your voice and loosen your tense muscles before speaking in front of your audience. I usually talk to myself in front of the mirror, changing my volume and pitch in the process. I also do simple exercises like neck and shoulder rolls to relieve my upper-body-muscle tension.

- **Deep Breathing**

Another great technique for relaxation that I practise is deep breathing. You need to take in deep breaths through your nose and hold it whilst you count to five. Then slowly exhale through your mouth, and whilst doing this, think about the pressure and nervousness that are slowly draining down your arms and out your fingertips and down your body and legs and out your toes. Repeating the procedure a few times can calm your anxieties.

- **Introduction**

Humour usually works to ease the tension in the room, so it is good to start with it as your speech introduction. Or you can start with a story that your audience can relate to.

Whichever way you choose, you have to be comfortable with it. The last thing you want is to overprepare on an introduction that will make you more anxious than ever!

- **Focus on Your Audience**

When your energy is shifted to your audience, i.e., focusing on their feedback, reaction, questions, and responses, your jitters will be gone.

- **Visual Aids**

Visual aids can increase your confidence when you speak and will provide a backup in case you forget what to say! They can keep you fully engaged in your presentation and make it a more interesting one. However, do not overdo on the visual aids as you might lose your focus to speak and maintain eye contact with your audience.

- **Positive Attitude**

It always boils down to your attitude at the end of the day; therefore, before facing your audience, you must ensure that positive energy flows within you. If you visualise yourself speaking confidently, you will become more confident. Positive imagery will allow you to develop a positive mental image of yourself. Having a positive mentality will, undoubtedly, allow you to perform at a higher level as compared with a negative mindset.

5.10 Put Yourself into Action

Some of the suggestions I have given above may or may not work with you. It is up to you to decide which one works best. Although the opinions of others are good for you to improve, it is you alone who can feel your nervous jitters or if you feel relaxed whilst speaking publicly.

Perhaps the most valuable tip to overcome your fear and anxiety in public speaking is to practise until you have gained all the confidence you need.

I fear not the man who has practiced 10,000 kicks once, but I fear the man who has practiced one kick 10,000 times. —Bruce Lee

CHAPTER 6

Connection

6.1 Introduction

Picture this: You did an amazing preparation for your speech. Your content materials were based on fantastic and up-to-date research. Your appearance was spectacular. You rehearsed your speech again and again. You had a great set of audience. You thought to yourself everything was on point, but alas, your audience seemed aloof and detached.

You then started questioning yourself. Did they understand you? Did they even hear you? Was there a disconnect somewhere?

Unfortunately, yes, there was.

Connection refers to actions that unite you with your audience. Throughout your speech and presentation, you have a bond with your audience, and it is all about how you engage with them and keep them involved and interested.

Feeling nervous during public speaking is common; however, having no connection with the audience whilst speaking is something that speakers should have greater concern for.

In this chapter, I will share several examples that you could use to keep your audience engaged during your speech presentations. Then again, different sets of audience respond differently; therefore, a good speaker will need to assess the audience, before and during the speech, to achieve a better sense of attachment with them.

6.2 Why You Need to Connect with Your Audience

'The speaker is so full of herself. She speaks right through us. It's as though we are of no importance to her. I don't like her style.'

'He must have given his speech hundreds of times to different sets of audience. He sounded like a robot. I have a feeling he just wanted to get the speech done and over with! I think that's a bit selfish.'

'I think he was trying too hard to bond with us, but it didn't work. Looked like there was a mismatch of interest between us and him.'

'She asked us to provide feedback on some of her questions, but they were too confusing. In the end, we got pretty exhausted trying to understand what she was trying to achieve. It was an exhausting session for the audience.'

'As an icebreaker, he started telling us the story of his life. But it got a bit too personal for some of us. Rather than making us feel comfortable, we felt otherwise!'

As a speaker, the above are examples of situations that we do not want to hear from our audience. These examples illustrate how important it is that we connect with our audience.

Let me explain further.

Connecting with your audience simply means that you are building rapport with them. Take for example a conversation that you are having with a friend or an acquaintance. For an ideal conversation to work, both you and the person you are talking to are having a two-way communication, and in the process, you are building rapport with each other.

Rapport building is important because it creates trust. As a public speaker, when you connect with your audience, they become more comfortable with you, and this means they are much more likely to pay attention to what you are saying. When they open up to you, it will be easier for you to gauge their feelings—what they want, what they need, and what they are expecting from you.

What happens when there is a disconnect? This means trouble, of course, because you do not get their attention and they will lose interest in you. Not only that, but they will also not bother respond or give feedback positively, or worse still, they will not even provide any feedback. Your hours of practice, your fantastic content, your awesome appearance—these will all go to waste. In conclusion, your speech will be a flop and all because you failed to have connection with your audience.

When you speak, you are physically, psychologically, and emotionally connected with your audience, and this produces a high level of trust which could produce a long-lasting impact on them. When you speak, it is not just about how good your materials are, how nice your jacket looks on you, or how much you have practised in front of the mirror before meeting your audience. In short, it is not about yourself.

Your audience is the stakeholder in this situation, and it is their needs that should be met. Your audience is interested in what you have to offer them, and for them to 'have this interest,' you must take on the task of ensuring that they are constantly engaged throughout your speech.

Do not fear your audience because when you regard them as a threat, you will be anxious and start to get defensive with them, which is the last thing you should do. It is a good idea to regard them as people you are having conversations with; that way, you are able to maintain a two-way communication with them, making them feel involved and appreciated for being there to listen to you speak.

6.3 How to Connect with Your Audience

The key here is to get connected and to stay connected. Notwithstanding this, do not take too long to warm up to your audience for fear that they have already lost interest in you and your speech.

I always believe that connecting with my audience begins even before I start my speech. Prior to the start of any event, I usually mingle and have casual conversations with several audience members, approaching them as they continue to gather. I find that this strategy works as the audience feels slightly relaxed even before I start my speech, which helps me connect with them more effectively.

Nonetheless, there may be certain occasions that do not allow you the liberty to mingle before the event starts. If situations like this occur, it is best that you do a quick background research of the audience so that you can be better prepared in how you intend to connect with them during your speech presentation.

When I speak to some of my audience members, I also pick up some of the things that they share with me; for example, their names, where they are from, their current interests, etc. I try to gauge as much as I can within the short chats that I have with them prior to my speech. Thereafter, during my speech, I am able to mention some of them in some relevant parts of my speech. I have to be careful, of course, not to make them uncomfortable in front of everyone else, and I only quote them just so that they would feel appreciated that I have included them in my speech.

I have observed that when I refer to my audience by name, it gives a sense of recognition and acknowledgement, and they feel valued to be part of my speech.

When giving your speech, you might become too engrossed in the content that you are delivering, so much so that you tend to lose focus on your audience. The best way to deal with this is to constantly keep track of the connection that you are having with them by introducing various ways and strategies to get them to stay connected to you.

You will need to master the art of asking them questions and responding to their questions without them feeling uncomfortable, upset, or dissatisfied. You will also need to ensure the feedback that you are providing them do not frustrate or provoke them in any way.

6.4 How to Ask Questions

One thing that speakers should be good at is, undoubtedly, to speak. However, there is a huge difference between speakers who just speak to their audience versus those who connect with their audience instead.

One of the ways to connect with your audience is to ask them questions. The common mistakes made by many speakers is that they either ask too much questions or they are overly eager to get answers from the audience. Your audience is not in an examination hall and desperately trying to answer your questions correctly. They are there to have their interests served, and it is your duty to ensure that their expectations are met.

Before anything else, warm up your audience to make them feel at ease. There are several ways to do this, which I will explain later in this chapter. When your audience feels comfortable with you, they feel that they know you, they trust you, and they are, therefore, willing to open up to you.

The challenge is to get your audience to be in an active mode and to stay in one. When you have developed rapport with them, ensure that they are continuously staying alert to you by asking them some questions.

You can start asking them questions in the early parts of your speech, but it is best not to launch tough questions that will make your audience slip away into boredom or into an 'exhausting zone.' Start with easy questions before you gradually move into thought-provoking ones. You should plan your questions well so that there is a continuity from one question to another.

You should also not take too long to start asking them questions. Like I mentioned earlier, you need to catch their interest whilst they are still 'warm' and their bodies and minds are still full of energy.

It is a good idea to tell your audience beforehand that you will be asking them a question. Catching them by surprise is not something that you want to do; otherwise, you will get blank looks from them as they have not been expecting questions from you.

When you do ask them, please ensure you ask them clearly and slowly. Questions should not be too complex as they might get all stressed up. There should also be a limit to the number of questions. We do not want your audience to be smothered by endless queries!

I believe the questions we ask our audience should be those that are fun, engaging, and interactive. That way, every audience member would want to participate instead of feeling worried that their name will be called up to answer a tough question!

When you get the answers from your audience, do not humiliate or make fun of them. When you ask them questions, you want them to gain knowledge and enjoy their time whilst doing so. It is not about making them feel bad or embarrassed for getting the wrong answers.

You need to be patient with your audience. Give them time to digest your questions. Control your emotions, and do not get irritated if they are not giving you speedy responses. Instead, guide them along to make sure that you do not 'lose' them in the process.

6.5 How to Answer Questions

When a speaker has ended his speech, his fears still suffice because this is the moment when the question-and-answer sessions begin. Speakers may feel that they have power over the audience; however, when it is time for the audience to start ask questions, many speakers feel that they are losing control.

I believe that the question-and-answer session is very vital to ensure that the audience has the opportunity to seek further clarification from the speaker. It will also provide a platform for the speaker to enhance some of his key points to the audience.

Therefore, when your audience asks you questions, do not feel annoyed or threatened. You should feel good that your audience is being responsive to you, and you should respond to them accordingly. However, there may be some situations where speakers are given a hard time by the audience because they are put on the spot to answer some questions which are difficult or sensitive in nature.

Keep in mind that when you answer questions from the audience, the bond between you and them is further strengthened, which means that they trust you more. It also further establishes your credibility as a subject-matter expert.

When you are asked a question, stay calm and focused. Listen to the entire question and understand it to the best of your knowledge. If you only choose to listen to perhaps an earlier or later part, or maybe even some parts of the question, you are not actually listening, and this will not help you answer the question effectively as you have already drawn premature conclusions on your response.

In addition, if you do not understand the question, you could seek clarification from the person who made the enquiry to ensure that you get the question right.

During a question-and-answer session like this, at times the speaker can be too immersed into a question that he tends to forget about the rest of the audience members. What you should do as a speaker is to include the rest of the audience by paraphrasing the question so that the rest can understand and be included in the session.

When you respond to a question, respond accordingly. It is not advisable to go all over the place just because you do not know how to answer it. The audience is observing you at all times, and they are able to detect your uncertainty and doubts, which can sometimes be clearly seen via your facial expressions and body language.

It is important to note that the person who asked the question should not be ridiculed in any manner, regardless of the question asked. Be polite in your response, do not get defensive, and do not get annoyed that a question has been put forth to you in such a manner. We do not want you to get into any form of debate with your audience! If you reply aggressively or defensively, you will be perceived to be a weak speaker, which could ultimately ruin an otherwise successful presentation.

If you happen to have a lot of information to share based on the question asked, try to avoid giving a mini-presentation to your audience. It is, after all, a question-and-answer session, and answers by you should be brief and concise. Nevertheless, encourage your audience to perhaps e-mail their questions to you so that you can attend to them accordingly. You can also suggest that they meet up with you during the networking session after the event is over, if the situation so permits.

6.6 How to Provide Feedback

Feedback is something that generates anxiety and fear; therefore, it is advisable to take careful steps when you wish to provide feedback to your audience.

The worry is this: You have delivered fantastic content to your audience, and they seemed extremely pleased with your presentation. They strongly believed that they have bonded with you throughout the session, and they have been a responsive and productive audience.

Imagine what they would feel if you provide them feedback which are negative and discouraging. This could cause them to eliminate all their good opinions of you as a speaker.

Bear in mind that offering feedback, albeit a constructive process in helping identify and resolving issues, is a tremendously delicate one. Feedback should be managed positively so that your audience feel valued and appreciated at the end of the session.

First of all, your feedback must be positive and encouraging. Choose your words wisely, and do not be mean. You should not belittle your audience or feel superior over them when you offer them feedback.

Second, it is best to be specific and clear when you speak to your audience for them to grasp what you are trying to convey. If you start beating around the bush, not only will you confuse the person you are giving feedback to, but the rest of the audience members will also be left baffled.

Third, get them to respond to you by asking 'what do you think?' after providing them with feedback. A two-way communication is a healthy way of connecting with the audience and ensuring that they feel comfortable throughout the session.

Finally, it is important to note that the feedback is intended to a person's comment or view, and not feedback on the person itself.

6.7 What You Need to Do to Maintain High-Impact Connection

Now that you have a bond with your audience, how are you going to maintain high-impact connection with them?

This is where you can start to get creative. You can apply various methods to maintain impactful connections with them. Check out some examples below:

'I liked the way he cracked jokes during some of the tougher topics of his speech. It lightened up an otherwise tense session.'

'He was a superb speaker! We could relate to the stories he shared with us. It made his presentation very interesting, and I even lost track of time. He was that good.'

'She was very generous with compliments whenever we gave her our comments. Made us feel appreciated.'

'I have heard many people speak, but this speaker managed to maintain an upbeat mood amongst the audience from start to finish! I wonder where he gets his energy. It was awesome!'

Before you even start your speech, it is advisable to determine who your audience is. This will make it make easier to not only involve them in your presentation, but also to help them better relate to the messages that you are conveying.

You have to care for the audience's needs, and you have to work towards meeting their expectations. This is what high-impact connection is all about.

Speakers usually start with good ice breakers to bridge the gap between him and the audience. Ice breakers are meant to help the audience relax and at the same time provide them the energy and motivation they need to stay connected with you.

The aim is for every audience member to feel that they are a part of your presentation.

6.7.1 Talk about the Interest of Your Audience

Yes, the speech is yours, and yes, you are the speaker. But no, it is not all about you. Some speakers tend to get a little bit excited with speaking, so much so that they worry they might not become the centre of attention if they move their focus on something or someone else.

Being self-absorbed in your speech will only make you lose your audience. They will get bored as you are not addressing their interests; rather, you are blindly conveying the message that you are trying to get across to them.

When you speak, talk about the interests of your audience. They are there to hear you speak about a specific subject matter, and they have dedicated their time and effort for you. What you should work on is to be interesting to them.

But how do you do this?

It is important to first know your audience, i.e., who they are and why they are there to listen to you. Give them what they want.

Do not pick and choose content just for the sake of giving an easy speech. You are there as an expert in your specific field; therefore, other people would like to hear your viewpoints, your suggestions, or your recommendations. They are not there just because you have ticked another item off your 'to-do list.'

Do not rush through a presentation just because you have done the speech so many times and that it was 'just another one' for you. Your 'just another one' could have been your audience's first or only opportunity, and think about how disappointed they will be if you are just delivering your speech just because you have to.

We think we are being interesting to others when we are being interesting to ourselves. —Jack Gardner, *Words Are Not Things*

6.7.2 Sense of Humour

I believe you agree with me when I say that laughter relieves our tension and stress. As a whole, it relaxes our body and keeps us at ease. As such, laughter is an important tool that you could apply as a form of stress release for your audience.

Well, how do you give your audience a warm welcome? Do you start laughing so that your audience laughs along? Do you tell them a string of jokes for the first half of your presentation? Do you get them to tell jokes and share with the rest of the audience?

Although humour is a fantastic way to catch your audience's attention, you have to be careful with the manner you are integrating it in your speech.

Maybe you have attended several presentations where the speakers try so hard to keep their audience entertained by cracking several jokes, but because the jokes were too cliché and unoriginal, the audience were left feeling far from fascinated.

Maybe you have experienced sessions where the speakers made fun of a few audience members just to get a few laughs from the crowd. This action will not only irk the audience as a whole, but they will also feel uncomfortable being there, and on top of it all, they will lose their respect towards the speaker.

You do not need to stress yourself and memorise a book of jokes just to impress your crowd. Being funny is not easy and is not a gift that every speaker has.

Remind yourself that you are there not to perform a stand-up comedy but to give a warm and friendly presentation to your audience. This way, you will feel more relaxed, and you can then focus on making yourself and your audience comfortable.

Remember, the audience reacts to you—your facial expressions, your body language, the way you speak—and when the timing is right, sprinkle your key points with a dash of humour to capture your audience's attention. Try it, it works for me!

A day without laughter is a day wasted. —Charlie Chaplin

6.7.3 Compliment the Audience

Praising someone will really make the person's day. It is human nature, after all, to crave for attention.

I truly believe that complimenting the audience is a wonderful way to connect with them. It makes them feel appreciated, and their interests will be captured. Above all, they will be in high spirits throughout my presentation, which makes them more connected to me.

The audience needs to be kept in a happy mood, and they constantly require encouragement and motivation to ensure that they comprehend your key points. The closer their association is with a speaker, the easier it is for the speaker to convey his messages to them.

How do you actually compliment your audience? There is an art to this, of course, and it is about showing them genuine appreciation. You have to mean what you say because if you do not do so, your audience will see right through your facial expressions and body language.

There is no need to be fancy with flatter words. Buttering up somebody for the sake of connecting with them is not the right way. Be simple with your compliments and use specific words. Being dramatic with language might seem like an act of overpraising, thus should be avoided.

It helps to be spontaneous because bad timing would only mean that you have pre-planned your compliments, and it might not be received well by your audience.

6.7.4 Tell a Story

I always believe that telling a story is the best ice breaker. Stories bring us back to moments where we are able to relate to our life and where the audience is able to relate to theirs too.

Your stories should make your audience feel relaxed and laid-back. You have to be honest in your stories, especially when it comes to your personal stories. However, avoid those that are too revealing, which would only make your audience feel uneasy or bored. You want your stories to captivate them, not drive them away.

Stories will also make people remember you. It gives you that personal touch with the audience. Notwithstanding this, it is not sufficient to share amusing stories because you would need to tell them stories that illustrate your key points and messages.

This is why you need to ensure your stories have a beginning and an end. When all is said and done, you do not want to leave the audience feeling confused about the purpose of your story or the message that you are trying to get across to them. Your audience should be interested in your stories as the message is relevant to them.

A good storyteller has creative skills. Set the scene and the characters clearly. Describe events distinctly. Be expressive. Be energetic.

Make your story relatable to your audience. I enjoy getting feedback from my audience that they are able to connect with my stories, which made my overall presentation very interesting to them.

6.7.5 Warm and Upbeat Mood

Please remember to start your session not just by looking energised, but also by actually feeling it.

It is vital to provide your audience with a comfortable environment within which they can respond positively to your messages.

Do not face your audience looking so uptight and feeling like you have a thousand regrets of being there. Do not speak to your audience feeling downbeat and looking all gloomy like you cannot wait to leave.

Some speakers are a natural when it comes to warming up with the audience; however, some others may find it slightly difficult to connect. Whether you fall in the former category or latter, the important thing is to develop an upbeat environment so that your audience impulsively feels the positive vibes around them, which, thereafter, encourages them to respond positively to you.

Your challenge is to warm up the room with your energetic and friendly presence. That is certainly a fantastic way to start an event. If your audience enjoyed the session so much that they did not even realise that you have been speaking for hours, you have done an awesome job!

6.8 Put Yourself into Action

Let me start by giving you a summary of what you have learnt so far:

Connecting with the audience refers to two-way conversations with your audience. You speak, they respond. They provide feedback, you respond. It might seem easy and straightforward; however, human interactions are not that clear-cut, and at times the connection is lost because of the actions or inactions of the speaker, whether done intentionally or otherwise.

Always begin your speech on a positive note, and make sure you really mean it. Honesty is crucial; however, it does not help if you are being too honest about what you are really feeling at the moment. For example, you did not start your day well. You were stuck in heavy traffic. You were caught up in bad weather. You missed your train. You had all sorts of problems and challenges before coming to meet your audience. If I was a member of the audience, hearing these from my speaker would sort of drain my mood as he had started his speech by sharing too many negative stories.

Take your time when delivering your speech, and do not rush; say your piece, and do not leave the audience high and dry.

Your voice must reflect passion and eagerness. Your facial expressions and body language must express that you are calm and relaxed. Have a good sense of humour and captivate the audience with your tales and narratives. Share the audience's concerns and offer them solutions to their problems.

Monitor your audience at all times. As soon as you observe that you are losing them, be creative and change the manner of your speech. Become a versatile speaker who is able to adjust and improvise his speech spontaneously.

If you make mistakes in your speech, do not panic because mistakes make you appear as someone real instead of a robot, and your audience might be able to relate to you better, hence strengthening their connection with you.

CHAPTER 7

Application of ABC Method for Leaders

Communication is a skill that you can learn. It's like riding a bicycle or typing. If you're willing to work at it, you can rapidly improve the quality of every part of your life. —Brian Tracy, International Speaker

Now that you have a much better understanding of the ABC Method, are you feeling all excited to start speaking in front of an audience?

Let us now imagine you are a newly-appointed team leader tasked to pitch an idea to your team members. Your presentation slides are ready, and you have rehearsed them several times. You have even bought yourself a new suit for the special occasion, and you are feeling very confident. You are now ready to step up on stage in front of a large audience.

From the side of the stage, you can feel a lot of energy coming from a room full of people you already know. You scan through their expressions, and you can see that they look excited and enthusiastic.

You heave a sigh of relief. This will be good.

Unfortunately, as soon as you step out on stage and face the audience, your confidence level starts to crumble. You suddenly become numb.

Your eyes start to dart around the hall, and you are now pacing up and down the stage, unable to control your nervousness.

You look at the audience. You notice that, at first, the audience is quiet, then they start murmuring at one another.

This is the moment when you tell yourself that you have landed in a very uncomfortable position—a place where no speaker and presenter should ever be—and you slowly start questioning your ability as a leader and a communicator.

Believe it or not, scenarios like these, i.e., where leaders speak disastrously in front of their audiences, are quite normal in many and different types of events around the world.

As a leader, you are expected to fulfil a leadership role that mostly involves interaction and communication with various parties from all levels and walks of life. There is no excuse for you to shy away from this as it is assumed that you should be able to speak and present well, especially if you are a leader representing your esteemed organisation.

As soon as you start speaking, your audience will start forming a perception whether they appreciate it or otherwise. Different audience members will evaluate you differently. Some might perceive you as a speaker who is articulate, competent, and confident, whilst some others might have a completely different and negative perception.

Think of it like this: As a leader who can effectively communicate with numerous audiences, it will not only allow you to engage with them at ease, but you will also be able to encourage them to become enthusiastic about their goals and aspirations. This will undeniably provide you with the support you need to achieve your desired outcomes.

A leader needs to articulate a compelling vision and drive others to work towards achieving it. For this to happen, clarity is key because distortions and misrepresentations during communication will only lead to the confusion of others.

Your topic of presentation might be a very important one, but it would not mean anything if your audience does not have any interest in it. The goal is for the audience to be mesmerised with the topic whilst at the same time feeling appreciated and cared for during your presentation.

The rule is simple: Your audience is equally, if not more important than the topic of your presentation. When you speak, it is for them to listen and not for your listening pleasure alone. When they listen, they need to understand and absorb what you have shared with them; therefore, it is also not for your speaking pleasure alone as well.

Getting carried away with your presentation is also out of the question because the audience will get restless and agitated, making it impossible for them to continue focusing on what you are trying to say.

It is always advisable to use simple and plain language when addressing your audience. You might be presenting a topic which requires the use of numerous technical jargons, and your audience can easily get 'lost' in your presentation. The way to keep them continuously engaged is by using sentences that are structured and precise. Always be honest with your audience and help them gain benefits from your presentation by sharing meaningful and valuable information.

Before I go on explaining how you can apply the ABC Method in your presentation, let us now look at some important characteristics of an effective speaker and an effective presentation.

Characteristics of an Effective Speaker

- Subject-Matter Expert

An effective speaker is very well informed of his presentation topic. He has done extensive research on the said topic and is able to provide up-to-date insights, address issues, and propose recommendations. A speaker's effectiveness will also be elevated if he has years of experience and exposure on the topic as well. If he has this quality, the audience will have a positive perception of him and will regard him as a credible speaker.

- Great Connection with the Audience

An effective speaker does not rush his audience. This means that good speakers take time to get to know their audience, try to learn their names and what they are expecting from the presentation.

There may be audience members who are not as open-minded in the sense that they might not be able to accept the speaker's views easily; however, an effective speaker will not be bothered by this fact. Instead of being upset, a good speaker respects the differences in the audience's opinions and perspectives because this is a fantastic way for the speaker to learn and improve.

As much as respecting the different viewpoints of the audience members, an effective speaker also respects that the audience comes from different backgrounds, cultures, and beliefs, which had shaped their thought process.

- Maintain Professionalism

A speaker is a professional in his given field, and an effective speaker is one who is able to maintain professionalism in all circumstances. He is able to keep his cool and not get easily distressed, especially when addressing some debatable questions put forth by the audience.

Effective speakers always encourage their audience to share and contribute their experiences as this allows the audience to feel calmer and more composed during the session.

- Highly Engaging

An effective speaker is capable of making his audience wanting for more. He comes across as a lively and enthusiastic speaker, using varieties of pitch, volume, and style when speaking. He uses facial expressions when presenting different sets of ideas, and his body gestures make the audience feel relaxed during the presentation.

Speakers who fall within this category are far from monotonous. They bring 'colour' to a presentation by making it interesting and thought-provoking. Despite the variety of expressions, styles, and gestures used, they are still able to speak articulately and provide the necessary takeaways that their audience is looking forward to receiving.

Some speakers prefer using audio and visual aids when illustrating their points across, whilst some others prefer not to. Either way, effective speakers are always able to understand the needs of their audience, and they make sure that they offer valuable and informative input to them. They are also able to see which audience member requires more attention or need to be more participative in discussions.

- Flexible and Compassionate

An effective speaker is flexible when he is able to adapt to various training plans and methods to give the best to meet his audience's needs. Good speakers can easily accommodate different user expectations, and they are also open to receiving new viewpoints and different perspectives.

Speakers might not have answers for every question posed to them by their audience, and at times they might not even be in agreement on some remarks made by their audience. However, a flexible speaker does not stay rigid in his thoughts; instead, he keeps an open mind and adapts to every situation in the best manner possible. He is also able to maintain his composure and does not present himself as being distressed by any questions, comments, or disagreements put forward by the audience.

An effective speaker also understands that certain topics may have an emotional impact on their audience. This is why a speaker needs to have strong empathy skills to recognise the feelings of others, which allows him to have better interaction with them.

- Continuous Professional Development

It is common for speakers to receive feedback from the audience after a particular session, and at times the feedback received might not be as positive as he had hoped for.

A speaker must always be open to criticisms, especially when it comes to the most important people in his session—his audience. Allowing yourself to be evaluated by your audience is a fantastic step to improve your skills and capabilities as a speaker.

All feedback should be critically analysed, and this way, speakers can continuously work towards improving themselves.

Be open to learn new skills, and treat everything as a learning process. Always use negative feedback as good feedback, i.e., use them as a form of advantage to become better in what you do.

Characteristics of an Effective Presentation

- Effective Learning Atmosphere

Without doubt, a conducive learning environment can be created if there is a positive atmosphere. A good speaker is able to build this atmosphere which is based on trust and understanding.

It is often said that it takes time to build and earn trust. If this is the case, how would a speaker then be able to get his audience to trust him given that he has only a limited time with them?

There are several ways for a speaker to do this:

- Maintain confidentiality at all times. This will ensure that the audience feels secure throughout the session, which, in turn, encourages them to express their thoughts freely.
- Feedback—constructive, not destructive. When the audience provides feedback, the speaker should take the necessary steps to address how important their feedback was to everyone as whole. This gives the audience a positive feeling that they are positively contributing to the session.
- Be positive at all times. Always be honest with your audience and provide them with constructive comments. Throughout a session, the audience might need to get a little motivation to keep them going. It is important for the speaker to observe the behaviour of an audience to ensure that every one of them remains positive throughout the session.

- Content Coverage

For a speaker, keeping to time is of utmost importance as it would be easy for the participants to follow through each part of the session in a logical manner. There must be a proper flow of content in the speaker's presentation.

Although the audience should be encouraged to contribute, there is a possibility that their concerns may deviate from the speaker's presentation topic. If a situation like this takes place, the speaker can offer to address their concerns during a break or during a specific Q&A session at the end. Acknowledging the concerns and remembering to address them is certainly a plus point for an effective speaker.

- Facilitation Skills

Every speaker should adhere to some basic facilitation strategies to help him achieve the desired outcomes of the session.

Speakers should ask open-ended questions to get the audience to provide more information; for example, their understanding of the subject and their true feelings on a particular issue.

When the speaker receives answers from the audience, he should listen to their contributions carefully and make an analysis of the response without judging the audience.

Should the speaker spot participants who are not 'on the same page' with the rest, he should not ignore them. Speakers should make their course materials clear and in a language that is easy for all to comprehend.

An effective presentation is one that is dynamic and lively and completed within a specified timeframe. Too lengthy a presentation will only make the participants become lethargic and weary.

- Well-Structured Handouts

A speaker's handouts may include PowerPoint slides, individual and group exercise worksheets, and other documents which are related to the speaker's presentation.

When preparing handouts for distribution to the audience, speakers must ensure that the handouts have been created with a learning goal. You do not want to confuse the participants by giving them a disorganised set of content for them to refer to.

You should also be selective with your handouts. At times less is more, and if there is no necessity to provide your participants with the handouts, you do not need to do so. The rule is to provide them with sufficient content that has a significant contribution to their understanding of your session.

Make sure your handouts are in an easy-to-read format, which means they need to have the appropriate font size and type for reading.

- Improve on Creativity

- Find out more about your audience before the actual presentation day. If you are unable to do so, spend a bit of time in the beginning of your session to ask some questions and encourage them to express their views on certain issues. This is one of the best ways to get an overview of the needs and expectations of your audience.
- If your session is scheduled for a rather lengthy timeframe, ensure you have breaks in between to allow your audience to have time to digest the information that you have shared with them. Having group exercises in between sessions is also an effective way to get the audience to unwind and be energised before continuing with the following session/s.
- It helps if you could personalise your presentation by sharing examples from your personal life, a sensational current topic, or case studies or by using metaphors and analogies. This makes it easier for the audience to relate to you and your presentation and gives them a sense of familiarity and understanding. Your audience will have that immediate connection with you, and they can keep an open mind throughout the session.
- It is also a good idea to keep a set of skeleton notes to refer to whilst speaking. Notes like this provide keywords or phrases that will trigger you with ideas to speak throughout your presentation. It allows your ideas to systematically flow whilst

at the same time give you an opportunity to express your ideas freely. It is not advisable to speak with a heavy prewritten script at hand as that shows your lack of confidence and credibility as a speaker.
- Visual aids can be appealing to certain participants, especially to those who are visual learners.
- An effective presentation is when the audience is left wanting for more. This is why it is best to end your session with a question for them to ponder.
- Analyse how you did from your session based on your own observations, formal evaluation from the audience, or informal discussions with observers of your session. Some speakers record themselves to review their own behaviours throughout the presentation.

Guidelines on the Application of ABC Method

The following are guidelines for you to use in the planning, preparing, and delivering of your presentation based on the ABC Method.

<u>Planning Your Presentation</u>

1. Audience

    - Who is your audience?
    - What does your audience have in common with you?
    - What does your audience have in common with one another?
    - What is your audience's needs and expectations?
    - What is the purpose of your presentation to the audience?
    - What are your desired outcomes from this presentation?
    - How long do you need to present to this audience?

2. Message

    - What is the most important message that you want the audience to remember out of your presentation?

3. Visual Aids

    - Will you use visual aids, and if yes, what types of visual aids will you use?

Preparing Your Presentation

4. Opening

    - Start with a warm introduction.
    - Capture the attention of the audience with a personal life story, a question, an analogy or metaphor, or an interesting current topic.
    - Give a preview of what the audience can expect from your presentation.
    - Share a little bit of yourself, not too much, but enough to catch their interest and give them a sense of confidence in your credibility.
    - Encourage feedback from the audience.

5. Presentation Body

    - Feel free to build your presentation around different themes, whichever suits your audience's needs and expectations. You can approach with a problem and suggest solutions, or you can approach with a case study and discuss possible issues, concerns, and recommendations.
    - Do not use old statistics and data. If you need to use any, make sure they are updated but do not overuse them.

- Illustrations using pictures, stories, and real-life examples work better than heavy fact-based data.

6. Conclusion

    - Summarise the main points and extract the key takeaways so that it is easier for the audience to comprehend.
    - Encourage the audience to apply what they have learnt in theory that day.
    - Finish your presentation on a positive note.
    - End on time.

Delivering Your Presentation

7. Delivery

    - Be clear and precise when speaking.
    - Do not use flowery language. Keep it simple and straightforward.
    - Speak in short phrases.
    - Technical jargon should not be overused, and if need be, translate the terms for better understanding.
    - Emphasise main points.
    - Manage the style, volume, and pitch of your voice.
    - Have an interactive session instead of having a one-way conversation.
    - Smoothly transition between ideas.
    - Respect your audience, be courteous with them at all times, and do not judge them based on their comments and responses.

8. Body Language

    - Look at the audience when you speak to them.
    - Work on the right facial expressions, body language, gestures, and postures.

- Do not pace around the room as it shows your nervousness.
- Stand instead of sitting down whilst you speak. When you stand, do not slouch because you will appear tired and weary.
- Use your hands whilst speaking, but do not overuse hand gestures as it might be distracting.
- Wear comfortable and proper attire.

9. Visual Aids

    - When you have visual aids, do not forget your audience. Some speakers get distracted by their own visual aids, and they end up losing eye contact with their audience.
    - Place the visual aids where they can be seen by everyone.
    - Use the visual aids only when they need to be used.
    - Check/test your visual aids before your session starts.
    - Add pictures to your visual aids instead of just words. If you do need to use words, make sure appropriate font type and size are used.

Below is a checklist on the application of the ABC Method in the planning, preparation, and delivery of your presentation as a speaker or presenter.

Checklist on the Application of the ABC Method

ASPIRATION
1. Establish the purpose of your presentation.
2. Establish the desired outcomes/objectives of your presentation.
3. Establish the structure of your speaking and presenting.
4. Research the common factors and differences amongst the audience.
5. Research the audience's needs and their expectations out of the presentation.
BEHAVIOUR
1. Maintain professionalism.
2. Speak with conviction.
3. Maintain a positive body language and personal appearance.
4. Be respectful, honest and courteous at all times.
5. Listen with empathy.
6. Deliver solid content with the expected deliverables and key takeaways.
CONNECTION
1. Ask your audience questions.
2. Talk about the interests of your audience.
3. Answer your audience's questions.
4. Compliment the audience.
5. Provide feedback to your audience and encourage them to provide feedback to you.
6. Share stories with them, and be very engaging and inspiring.

The Planning, Preparation, and Delivery of Your Presentation

Delivery
1. The speaker greeted the audience warmly.
2. I could hear the speaker.
3. I could understand the speaker.
4. The talk was delivered with warmth and feeling.
5. The talk was delivered with personal conviction from both the speaker's mind and heart.
6. The presentation seemed practiced.
7. The speaker involved the audience.
8. The speaker handled questions and comments with calm courtesy.
9. The talk contained effective examples and illustrations.
10. The speaker defined technical terms and statistics for us.
Contents
1. The opening got my attention.
2. The introduction told me what to expect from the presentation.
3. The objective of the talk was clear.
4. The talk was designed in a logical way from beginning to middle and end.
5. The presentation was well-suited to the audience.
6. The content was interesting to me.
7. The speaker summarised the main points before finishing.
8. The speaker let us know when the talk was over.
9. The talk ended on a strong final line with a clear Call to Action (CTA).
10. The speaker ended on time.

Body Language
1. The speaker stood during the presentation.
2. The speaker had good eye contact with the audience.
3. The speaker showed no distracting movements or gestures.
4. The speaker smiled.
5. The speaker used his/her hands to help communicate ideas visually.
6. The speaker tried to use verbal focusing techniques.
Visual Aids
1. The speaker used visual aids.
2. I could read the material from where I was sitting.
3. The visual aids got the point across in a clear and simple way.
4. The speaker did not block the screen or flipchart.
5. The speaker talked to the audience rather than to the screen or flipchart.
6. The visual aids used key words rather than sentences.

CHAPTER 8

Personal Development Plan

8.1 Why You Need to Have a Personal Development Plan

Now that you understand what I mean when I say that you need aspiration, behaviour, and connection to become a high-impact speaker and presenter, I want you to ask yourself these questions:

What is it that I really want to achieve?

How am I going to achieve it?

When am I able to achieve it?

Do you have the answers to the above questions? Perhaps you do, or perhaps you are unsure if your answers make sense. My advice for you now is to start developing a personal development plan that is specifically tailored to you, your wants, and your needs.

Do you know what a personal development plan is?

On a daily basis, you make different kinds of plans; for example, what time to leave for work, how many grocery items you need to get, or what you will be having for dinner.

However, you might have missed some important aspects as to how a proper plan really works. For example, perhaps you did not set targets on how you plan to achieve each item that you had planned for.

A personal development plan is a structured action plan that specifically refers to your personal development goals, in this particular case, to become a high-impact speaker and presenter. It is a refined document that allows you to set your own personal targets and how you find the best methods towards achieving them. A good personal development plan describes approaches on how you could improve your skills and manage your growth as a high-impact speaker and presenter.

Having a personal development plan means that you can identify every single goal that you want to achieve and have your own strategies on how to achieve them within a desired timeframe. You need to think through each goal as there could be different methods and deadlines towards achieving them. Some goals could be very simple, whereas some others may require a lot more time, effort, or financial resources.

It is, therefore, very crucial to know what you really want. Many people think they do know; however, in the process of achieving what they want, they face struggles and challenges that they had not planned for. A personal development plan guides you to your destination, specifically itemising the obstacles that you will be facing along the way.

With a proper plan like this, your dream will not only remain a dream. It brings clarity to your line of thoughts, which means that you will know exactly what you want to achieve.

Don't you think a plan like this would give you a clear sense of direction and relieve you of your stress and concerns?

8.2 How You Develop Your Personal Development Plan

Take time when you design your personal development plan because it is a very important document that should not be rushed through. Do not take too long, however, as you will start procrastinating and end up not completing it!

Let me show you how easy it is to develop a personal development plan. I have identified three main steps which I feel are essential towards the process.

Step 1: Identify Your Goals

Always begin something with the end in mind. That way, you will not get 'lost' in your own journey. You may make mistakes along the way, and there will be lessons learnt in the process; however, bear in mind that mistakes make you lose out on your resources. If potential mistakes can be detected early during your planning process, they are best to be avoided.

Because of this, you need to have clarity in your vision. Think about what is ahead for you and be honest with yourself and your capabilities.

For example, to become a high-impact speaker and presenter, your goals could include the following:

 a. Practise how to manage my emotions when interacting with my audience
 b. Develop confidence whilst speaking and presenting
 c. Develop skills to listen with empathy

Step 2: Identify Your Deadlines and Milestones

Be very practical in determining your respective timeframes.

When you plan your goals, it is natural for you to get a little bit excited to achieve them. In the process, you might place deadlines and milestones which do not make so much sense based on the support and resources you have or on your strengths or weaknesses.

I advise you to select a deadline or milestone that is feasible and realistic for each goal that you plan to achieve. The important thing to note is to not get overly enthusiastic or too pessimistic. If you strongly believe that your desired outcome can be attained within one month, then be brave enough to plot the deadline in your personal development plan, and do not stretch the timeframe just because you feel that you needed more time for it.

Then again, if your goal can only be attainable within a year, for example, you should not rush through by charting a much earlier deadline as this will only make it impossible for it to be achieved.

Step 3: Identify Your Resources/Support

Now that you know your destination and when you need to be there, the next step is to see what you need with you in the journey. Do you have the required skills and expertise? Do you have all the support and resources you need? During this planning phase, you need to start thinking of ways and methods that could help you along the way. Whilst listing them out, do a SWOT analysis, i.e., bear in mind your strengths, weaknesses, opportunities, and threats that could either assist or hinder your movement forward.

Do not compare your result with others, although it might be similar to yours. How they approach their goal could be way different from how you should be approaching yours. For example, their support system or availability of resources and yours could be poles apart. This is why the destination is the same for many people, but the journey is different for all.

8.3 What You Need to Do to Maintain a High-Impact Personal Development Plan

Once your personal development plan is in place, and you have started using it, do not regard it as just a one-time document. Instead, it is supposed to be a dynamic document as everything around you are changing.

The plan was correct when you first laid it out; however, as you move along in your journey in your quest to reach your destination, some activities and requirements may require change and modification.

Therefore, the document needs to be constantly reviewed and your goals are to be updated accordingly. This would ensure that you have a high-impact personal development plan that is functioning and effective. Life changes at a quick pace, hence the importance to review and adapt to it.

When is the best time to review it? I believe reviews are best done on a quarterly basis, just to be sure that your goals are still on track. Reviews should not be done too frequently as you may lose sight of what you plan to achieve. You may start to get anxious, and ultimately, you may even stop believing in your personal development plan!

Do not be afraid if there are drastic changes that need to be done. Focus on your result, and work towards completing the process.

It is also a very good idea to have your personal development plan validated by your mentor or coach to get feedback on your draft.

You may think that it is your personal plan and that you are the best person to prepare it; however, feedback from another person, especially from someone who is trained to review and validate documents like this, is extremely crucial to ensure that your plan is a workable one, not merely a 'one-way street' type of document.

8.4 Put Yourself into Action

You are now at your comfort zone where you feel safe and in control of yourself. With a personal development plan, you can move your way forward into your growth zone where you will then be able to say 'Yes! I have conquered my objectives, and I can now set new goals to achieve.'

Along the way, you may face a lot of fears and challenges, but with the plan serving as a guide, you would have expected some of them, and you would have already known how to overcome them. It will be a learning process for you, and ultimately, you will learn to deal with problems or issues that come your way.

I would say that a personal development plan is a structured document that will benefit you in various ways for both your personal life and professional life.

It brings clarity and focus into your life, and because of that, your ideas are clearer and well defined, you are more positive and productive in your undertakings, and you work hard and smart towards getting your skills enhanced to gain your future expectations.

I have shared below a personal development plan template that has the basic columns for you to list out your goals, support/resources required, and the respective deadlines for the goals.

It is advisable to include a column that states 'Updates as of (date)' for you to keep track of goals that are pending/in progress during that particular date.

I have separated the goals column into three—short-term goals, medium-term goals, and long-term goals—so that from an initial stage, you have already identified your priorities. I have also included an example so that you can see what you need to plot for each column.

Remember, do not be afraid to make mistakes whilst designing your personal development plan. Consult your friends, colleagues, superiors, family members, and those who are familiar with the process.

Template: Personal Development Plan

No.	Short-Term Goal	Deadline	Strength/Opportunity	Weakness/Threat	Resource/Support	Updates as of (date)
1						
2						
3						
	Medium-Term Goal					
1	Develop confidence whilst speaking and presenting	June 20xx	Register with Toastmasters to practise my public speaking and improve my communication skills	Lack of knowledge about the Toastmasters Club	Enquire from work colleagues who are members of the club	In progress
2						
3						
	Long-Term Goal					
1						
2						
3						

CHAPTER 9

10 Tips for High-Impact Speaking and Presenting

At one point or another in our lives, there is a possibility that we need to speak well in front of an audience; therefore, we should not take things lightly and leave things to chance.

Here are 10 effective tips on how you can speak and present with the kind of impact you need.

Tip no. 1: Where to Look When You Speak

When you are giving a presentation or speech, your body language and how you hold yourself in front of a crowd speaks to your audience as much as your words do. Part of not being nervous when you are speaking is by not 'acting' nervous. If you have complete control over your body, face, and hands, you can be calm and relaxed in front of other people, and you will eventually begin to feel more at ease as you perform your speech.

A common problem amongst speakers is 'how they use their eyes' when speaking to the audience. It is normal for a speaker to glance at his speaking notes or speech outline throughout a presentation to not get lost or have that terrifying feeling of not knowing what he is to say next. Even experienced speakers refer to their notes whilst speaking.

The problem with this approach is that as a public speaker, you have been asked to give a speech, not reading from your speech notes. Many adults also take offence at being read to. An audience wants to hear 'from' you and not just to hear you read 'to' them. If that was the only value of a public presentation, you could just hand out your speech as a white paper for their reading pleasure. However, this is not as effective as speaking, particularly if the purpose of your speech is to convince or to sell an idea/concept/product to your audience.

Therefore, the question now is, where should a speaker look to when he gives his speech? Many speakers tend to focus on a spot in the back of the room because looking at the audience's faces make them nervous. This strategy is better than staring down at your papers the whole time. One thing for sure, projection plays a big part in getting your message out, and even if you are using a microphone, if you speak 'out' into the crowd rather than speaking 'down,' your voice will be clearer, and you will naturally be able to use your diaphragm to better enunciate each word.

The other value of looking at a particular spot at the back of the room, i.e., the wall, is that it will help you project your voice, particularly if you are not using any form of amplification. The old actor's motto of 'performing to the last row' applies here because it means you consider everyone in the hall to be your audience and not just the people on the first row.

Notwithstanding the strategy above, one of the most valuable ways you can really connect with your audience and get your message across is to make eye contact with them. Eye contact is commonly used by salespeople to create a bond with their customers wherein this bond helps them with closure of sales.

Eye contact makes your audience look at you. It keeps them attentive. To use eye contact to its maximum value, move your eyes from one audience member to another, and speak to that individual directly. That eye contact can actually be felt by everyone around that particular individual, and it attracts other listeners to you too. Avoid lingering on one person because you do not want to stare at someone too much until it creeps the person out. By becoming skilled at using eye contact as you speak to a crowd, you are taking control of the presentation. Having control is a big key to success in speaking.

Tip no. 2: Create a Problem and Then Solve It

How well your presentation goes the next time you step up to a podium depends on several factors. One factor you can control is your script. The way you organise your content and how you present it to the audience can either totally captivate them and drive them step by step towards a conclusion, or it can simply bore them to sleep. It all depends on how you construct your presentation and how you present what you want them to know.

The difference between a great talk and a boring one is simple: A great talk is compelling. A great talk gets to the heart of a common experience. It addresses something we all go through and deals with a need we all experience. In short, a great talk solves a problem. To create a speech that reaches out and grabs the attention of your audience and holds them for the entire time of your presentation, you have to create a problem for them, and thereafter, you have to solve it.

When is the best time to create the problem? In your opening comments, of course. Do not shy away from being a bit melodramatic in your opening. Remember that the goal of the opening is to grab the audience's attention to interest them on your talk. You will need to present the problem statement in a personal way, i.e., meaningful on a personal level to the audience and to you. Focus about 20% of your time on the creation of the problem statement. By the time you have created it, your audience will be ready for you to guide them towards the solution.

With the audience 'in the palm of your hand,' you can now move directly to the description of a perfect solution. This can be broken down into two parts. First, describe what the perfect solution would look like. You do not need to bring up the solution just yet. Base your description of the perfect solution on the problem statement so that you have an aspect of the solution that fits every possible problem which you have created in the beginning of your talk.

The next phase comes in at approximately 50% into your speech time. Now that you have captured the audience's interest, use about 30-40% of your total time on the proposed solution, fitting it perfectly into the discussions revolving around the problem and an outline of what a perfect solution would look like. By this time, the audience is eager to know the solution, and all you have to do now is close the deal.

If we adhere to a standard 'term paper' approach to a programme, the final phase would be to sum up and go over what you had just talked about; however, we are not going to follow this model because it is the time for 'pay off'. Hence, in your closing statements, you will now need to finally disclose the action/s to be taken. By sharing with your audience what they can do in taking the first step towards putting your solution into motion, you are cashing in on all that energy that you have created in the first 80% of your speech.

The next step now is to close the deal by giving the audience concrete and 'right now' things that they can do to recognise the problem and start the wheels turning by making the solution a reality. If it is possible to do so, make the first step of implementing the solution right there in the room with the audience. These include signing up for a newsletter, getting their e-mail addresses, or going to a separate room for further counselling and discussion with them. By using this energy, you would have been able to convert passive listeners into active participants and all these with a very well designed and executed presentation plan.

Tip no. 3: Do Not Fear the Pause

Focus on how experienced speakers speak, and you will be able to observe how their content steadily flows throughout their presentation. It is a good exercise to use every opportunity you have to listen to different speakers and to learn from them. If the speaker is ineffective, observe their weaknesses and learn how to correct them so that you can improve your own presentation. If the speaker is good, observe their strengths and see how you can utilise their methods when you conduct your presentation.

When a speaker 'holds his audience in the palm of his hand,' the speaker will undoubtedly feel relaxed. This form of calculated relaxation achieved by the speaker is through the use of different speaking methods, such as hand gestures, vocal range, eye contact, etc. These actions should all be carefully planned by the speaker and can be perfected through time and practice.

You need to learn how to use pauses when speaking. Experienced speakers will often pause for dramatic effect to create interest amongst his audience or to put a point across. During intentional pauses like these, speakers can also check their notes or take a breather before starting to speak again.

Use pauses to your advantage. A pause is actually a very powerful communication tool that can be mastered and used wisely during your presentation. It is especially important if your speech is lengthy and technical and useful to avoid the audience's minds from wandering or to ensure that they do not doze off as you speak.

When you begin to use pauses and changes to the tempo of your presentation, you break the natural rhythm of your talk. The pause will jar the audience back to you, and they will suddenly be attentive with that 'what did I miss' look on their faces. That, in itself, is a real tool for you to help your audience stay focused and to be used particularly when you are approaching a significant point in your speech.

So the next time you are faced with a pause whilst speaking to your audience, do not fear. Just remember not to overuse it as it might irritate your audience and make them lose focus for the rest of your presentation.

Tip no. 4:

The software application Microsoft PowerPoint has been a revolution amongst speakers and presenters, specifically in the world of business. PowerPoint is not only reliable and easy to use, but also available with almost every implementation of the Microsoft Office suite. If you can use Microsoft Word, there is a high possibility that you will have the skills to put together an effective set of presentation slides using PowerPoint.

But just like anything else, there is the right way of using PowerPoint as a speaking tool, and there is also an incorrect way. The tool can be as much of a curse as it is a blessing to the speaker; therefore, it is always good to adhere to a set of guidelines on how to use PowerPoint to improve your presentation instead of worsening it.

When designing your slides, think about the problems that may arise in the course of your presentation. For one thing, it is a good idea not to put too much text on each PowerPoint slide. Long paragraphs of information on the screen will only cause your audience to squint when reading, or they might not even read it all. If you still need to reference your speech to your slides, perhaps you can just make your audience listen to you whilst you do so. Either way, part of your message will be lost as they try to keep up with you, and this has proven to be an ineffective way of using PowerPoint slides.

PowerPoint comes with interactive effects and animations. Notwithstanding this, avoid the temptation to go overboard with these dramatic effects. Although it is always nice to have a little humour in your presentation, but if your slides are overly tacky, it reduces the credibility of your talk. Furthermore, if every slide uses a different special effect, i.e., colour scheme or font, not only is that distracting to the audience, but it also makes you look like you have just discovered PowerPoint and had to play with all the toys it has to offer. You will appear to be a novice, and it might impact your reliability as a speaker. It is best to establish some form of standard and consistency for each slide.

Another great device that PowerPoint offers is to allow the software to change slides for you on a timed progression. This means that you can change a slide, for example, every two minutes, thus allowing you enough amount of time you want in between slides. Whilst this is also very slick, it is a dangerous toy to use because it can cause you to stumble whilst doing your talk. You have to have your talk planned to a high level of precision to pull this off. If you pause too much, or get a question from the audience, or experience any form of disruption, the slides will move on when you are still not supposed to; therefore, use this feature with caution and only if you feel at ease to do so.

Above all, do not turn your back to the audience when referring to/reading from a PowerPoint slide. This is the number one most common mistake people make. Turning your back to your audience is always a bad idea. If you must discuss the contents of the slide, do so facing the audience. Turning your back whilst looking and reading from your slides can be seen to be insulting and might also bore your audience.

Bullet points have proven to provide a much clearer message in comparison with a slide with heavy texts. This approach assures that PowerPoint remains a tool that you are using instead of a tool that is using you.

Tip no. 5: Illustrate, Illustrate, Illustrate

When a speaker loses an audience, too often it is a mystery to him. It is not, however, any mystery to the audience. The simple fact is that many speeches we listen to are heavy in content on a particular theory or idea. It is natural for us as humans to have trouble focusing on them long before losing interest. This is one of the many reasons speakers should be creative and use lots of stories and illustrations to make sure they hold the audience's attention.

The common mistake made by speakers is to look down on the needs of the audiences. By expressing his views and ideas via specific illustrations, speakers can better reach out to their audiences.

The use of stories and humour should get started as soon as the talk begins. One of the problems on public speaking has to do with the speed of processing. Science has proven to us that the human mind can think at least 10 times faster than it can hear. This means that for 90% of the time you are talking to a group, their minds have time on their hands. If you give them a concrete story to work with, the details of that story give that excess brain power something to do.

By opening with a light-hearted illustration, you capture the minds of your audience quickly. The best kind of an opening story is a humorous one, particularly if it is an anecdote from your past. This method not only is a wonderful way to get your talk off with an enjoyable story, but it also connects the audience to you and opens you to them, which, in turn, creates a bond and trust. When selecting a perfect opening humorous story, use two criteria to select just the right illustration. First, select a story that links to the problem to be solved by the presentation. If the problem is an abstract tone, such as spiritual hunger or political theory, that can be tricky. Try to get close to the illustration, or at least close enough, so that you can have a transition ready to take the audience from the story to the concept you wish to discuss first.

Second, connect your opening story and every illustration in your talk to your theme. By doing this every step of the way, the illustrations reach out to the audience, rescue them from drifting away from your presentation, and smoothly bring them back to the talk and what you want them to be thinking about at this part of your presentation.

You can tell if your audience is drifting away. Their eyes are looking away. They are fidgeting in their seats. They look bored. They are trying hard not to fall asleep. Clearly, these are all circumstances where they are losing interest in what is being said! If you observe these things happening, you must realise that you have probably spent too much time on theoretical ideas and that you would need to quickly think through a different mix of ideas and illustrations and execute them for the balance of your presentation.

A good illustration will at least keep the audience involved in the discussion, but a great illustration will actually become part of the presentation so you can tell the story and proceed to use elements of the story as the following points in your conceptual talk. When that works well, you will stop losing the audience because the story serves to anchor the rest of the presentation perfectly.

Therefore, learn the art of telling a good story. Great storytellers will teach us that the heart of a good story is in its details. But in a speaking setting, a story should be brief but easy to understand. A good story not only has humour, but it also has 'personality.' This helps compel the audience to connect to the talk and understand the ideas that you want them to grasp.

Tip no. 6: Maintaining Focus in Speaking

A speaking situation can be intimidating for even the most seasoned professional speakers. When speaking to a live audience, you really never know what is going to happen. Not only is there a possibility of freak occurrences of problems with the audience and the room, but you as a human being could also be subject to momentary memory halts that often come as the result of nervousness or by just looking up and seeing all those eyes looking back at you.

Much of the discipline of giving a public presentation is to establish an internal structure to your talk that helps you stay focused on your task and the subject of your presentation throughout your speaking duration. That structure can also be of huge value in helping you gauge your time and make adjustments for you to get the most crucial parts of your talk presented within the allocated timeframe even if that means leaving out less important parts of your presentation.

Majority of speakers live by a simple directive that gives a fine guideline for that structure:

- Tell them what you are going to do.
- Do what you said you were going to do.
- Tell them you did it.

This simple outline may be overly simplistic, but it is the heart of what makes a good presentation work. The simplicity of it also helps you stay focused under the pressure of a speaking situation. Any tool that can do this is a good tool.

During opening comments, tell the audience what they need to expect. At this point, you can share your personal information, greet the audience, and perhaps start with some light humour to set the tone of the talk. After you have gotten the speech underway, it is common to establish what the topic of your talk will be. But to do that, the most effective device is to make a statement of the problem. By phrasing the subject matter as a compelling and real problem to your audience, that creates interest as the audience will be thinking in their minds, 'Yes, I have that problem. Tell me how you will help me fix it.'

This is where you tell them what you are going to do. The body of your speech is usually between a three-to five-point discussion of the solution to the problem. It is advisable not to give them the entire heart of your speech but to let them know the ground you are about to cover. Not only does this give the audience a road map of what to expect, but it also lets them know that you are aware of what you are doing and when you will get it done. This gets rid of a secret fear of a speaker who is not in control of his presentation—something that would be dreaded by the audience!

Once you establish this roadmap for the rest of your speech, this gives the audience a good feel for where you will be going. By giving them this information early on, that actually reduces the impulse to interrupt you because they know you have a path to follow and they do not want to take you off it. It is now just a matter of stepping through each of the outlined areas and offer a solution to the problem statement. Naturally, your detailed discussion will have more content than your brief preview. But if you continue to broadcast to the audience where you are on the outline and that you are on track to reach the goal, that keeps them interested and keep them assured that the content that will be shared with them comes in an organised form.

It is always good to let the audience know when you are entering your closing statements. Many speakers use a simple clue like 'Let me point out . . . ' or 'I am closing with this . . .' to give the audience the signal that the presentation is almost done. This is common courtesy and a professional way to conduct a presentation. If you treat the audience with respect like this by telling them what you are going to do, by doing it, and finally telling them you have done it, it is easier for you to get good reviews and be invited back for more presentations.

Tip no. 7: Make Them Laugh

In the delightful Broadway musical *Singing in the Rain*, there is a song titled 'Make them Laugh,' which is based on the idea that the best way for any stage performer to build a bond with an audience is to use humour to bring a smile, or a laugh, to the audience. This is not just valid for stage performers. It is just as true when you begin to develop your style as a speaker.

If you pick up any self-help guide on how to become an effective speaker, one of the golden rules is to open with a joke, but guess what? This is not a hard and fast rule. Humour is the type of thing that works just as well about a minute into your presentation, halfway through, or just about anywhere during your presentation when you feel you are losing your audience.

Audience psychology is a funny thing, ironically, not in the 'laughter' sense. The truth is that when you first begin to speak to an audience, they are probably listening to you. People usually have a slight curiosity about you and what you have to say and will take interest in you if for no other reason than you are a new person up there in front of them. Whilst it is certainly not a bad idea to open with humour, observe the audience for their reaction to your presentation. They need a joke when you can see their heads nodding or their eyes drifting. That is when humour brings the audience back to you and hooks them back into your presentation.

The biggest problem with a lot of speaking situations is that you may be presenting ideas to the audience. Whilst an idea is a good thing, people have trouble staying focused on pure concepts for very long. Most good speakers use illustrations, stories, and humour to keep the audience focused on what they are talking about. This is where a generous use of humour will help the speaker's speaking style as well.

Humour has a certain effect on the human psychology that causes the listener to bond with the speaker in a unique way. Simply put, using humour in your presentation makes people like you. When your audience likes you, they want to hear what you have to say. There is just no getting around the fact that people will listen to, accept, understand, and make their own ideas presented with humour far more readily than if your talk is a dry presentation of material, even if it is important material.

But what if you do not know how to use humour? You can always just tell a joke; however, canned jokes are just that, i.e., attempts to use someone else's humour. They do work (if it is a good joke, of course), but if the humour is irrelevant to what you are talking about or to you as a speaker, often it is not as effective as it should be. The best humour is actually self-deprecating remarks as you speak. These are easy to come up with by simply using yourself as the subject of an illustration. For example, if this topic was part of your speech, you might say, 'You know, it's easy to get tongue-tied and bumble around up here trying to use humour. But you folks won't make a mess of it like I am doing.'

The above example is not even a very good joke, but because it is highly relevant, it is self-deprecating, and it serves as a light moment in the presentation, it will probably get a chuckle from the audience. A chuckle is really all you are looking for. You are not trying to become a stand-up comic up there. Humour that is too wild and designed to bring about a hearty laughter from the audience can actually be distracting. You just want little asides that are of a humorous nature to bring your audience back to listening to you.

Listen to good speakers you admire and take notes on how they seem to slip in and out of humour easily and effortlessly and how quickly that builds rapport with the audience. It will take some practice to get good at using humour as you speak, but it will improve your presentation style tremendously, and isn't that the whole idea?

Tip no. 8: Speak Using More Than Your Voice

One of the misperceptions on the term 'speaking' is that the technique of becoming good at speaking is all in how you speak. The truth is that your voice is only part of what you need to be successful in giving a presentation to a group of people. To become an effective public speaker, you should use every resource you have, including your body language, your arms, and your legs, to capture the attention of the crowd.

There is nothing more boring than a speaker who stands in one place, who never makes any hand gestures, and who monotonously speaks. To avoid this so-called curse, express yourself better with facial expressions, gestures of your arms and body movements, because that extra effort is what can make a fair presentation good or a good presentation better.

A public presentation can be compared to eating a meal in a restaurant. A good chef knows that there is more to fine dining than just preparing and offering food because it should also come with great service and ambiance to ensure that the presentation of the food makes the meal delightful to eat. The same is true of a speaking situation. It is not enough for a speaker to stand in front of his audience to speak out the information. A speaker will only be impactful when he is <u>communicating to the audience,</u> and this is achieved when his audience has a grasp of what he is saying.

Body movement is probably the most underused speaking method, but it is also one of the most effective. When you speak to an audience, do not just stand in one place. Move away from the lectern (if you are using one) and walk around a bit, perhaps from one side of the podium to the other. Use your hands to help you describe an illustration or to gesture with emphasis towards the crowd when your text fits that kind of expression. This movement is good for you because it is a way of walking off your nervousness. It is good for the audience too because it keeps them interested. Plus, it is a powerful way for to get your point across to them and assure you that you are being understood.

The relationship between speaking and public performance is unmistakable. The key word here is the audience 'watches' the speaker. Taking in the presentation of a speaker is an event that brings in all the audience's senses. The more the audience actually 'experiences the speaker' rather than just hears out what the speaker has to say, the better they will like the presentation and the more likely they will be to agree with what the speaker has to say or take action in the direction the speaker had hoped they would.

Undeniably, once you start using body movements on stage, there is always a risk of accidents. For example, swinging your arms to emphasis a point might cause you to knock something over. You could trip over a microphone cord and be in danger of falling down. Your wardrobe could malfunction because of the increased stress. Speaking is a live event, and however frequent you have rehearsed for it, some accidents still happen when you least expect it! Ensure you evaluate the speaking setting so you are aware of potential causes of accidents, and be mentally prepared respond to whatever surprises that may come your way.

The other risk is that by stepping away from the lectern, you step away from your speech notes and outline, which are usually placed on the lectern. To enable yourself to wean away from having to have the notes and outline in front of you all the time, select one or two sections where you do not need to refer to the documents. Perhaps use that time to share a personal story with your audience, something that you do not need to refer your notes and outline with. Your movements will then be confident and effective, and you will then be able to make an easy transition back to the lectern to start speaking on the following section of your presentation.

Tip no. 9: Tell Them Something They Do Not Know

When an author is trying to come up with a topic for his next story or novel, old pros in the writing game will always give him the same advice: 'Write about what you know.' This is because if you speak from your own area of expertise, you will speak with authority and passion, and these not only make for a great story or novel, but they are also useful criteria for a really good speaking event.

When you are putting together what you will use for your talk to a particular group that you want to amaze, you want both the elements of authority and passion. But on top of that, you have to give them something to make it perfect. Tell them something that they do not know to achieve a right balance between something that is familiar versus something new and fascinating.

Sometimes telling them something they do not know might be as simple as sharing a new joke that they have not heard. You can also share a fascinating story or anecdote that will lead directly into your talk, i.e., something that can grab their attention and let them know that this is going to be an interesting take on the subject. Finding jokes that nobody has ever heard before can be a challenge; therefore, it could be better to find a funny or amusing situation that relates to a topic from your past. By telling them a story of that situation with plenty of self-referencing humour and commentary, you will leave your audience very amused as you enter the next part, i.e., the body of your speech, but at the same time retaining their interest in you and your topic.

Sometimes finding material that is new to your audience is obvious and easy to identify. You might have been invited to speak because of your subject-matter expertise. For example, if you are giving a speech on how to make your own PC from scratch, and you are an expert on the matter, you are then in a good shape right off the bat.

If your topic is on current affairs, you will need to get updated insights to raise some eyebrows in the room. A rich repository of little-known facts lies in what we call trivia and urban myth. Let me give you an example. Let us say you are giving a talk about the Internet. There is a strong possibility that your audience knows quite a bit about the Internet; however, with a little bit of research, you can uncover a lot of trivia about how the Internet came to be, how the Internet actually works at a structural level, or if Al Gore really did invent it. (Fun fact: He didn't!)

The Internet is a great avenue to pull in dozens of urban myths that will make for a very enjoyable presentation, from how viruses work to if that African prince will really be sending you $5 million. (Unfortunately, he will not!)

When researching for your speech topic, ensure that it not only has solid content, but that it should also include interesting information, amusing stories and anecdotes that could give the audience something to talk about during refreshments/coffee breaks. A memorable speech would make them want you to come back to speak.

Tip no. 10: When Things Do Not Go as Planned

Public speaking is a live event, and this means that just about anything can happen in the middle of your presentation—an interruption, a distraction, or some form of disturbance. To change your fear of the unexpected, think ahead and see what you need to do if such a thing would come up and how you will get the crowd back on track in the presentation.

Depending on how you conduct your presentation and the type of gathering, questions or objections received from the audience, situations like these could potentially take you off course. This is especially true if you did not plan to have an open-forum type of discussion. For example, if you set out doing your talk as a speech and not a discussion and someone interrupts, the first thing to do is recognise the audience member who had interrupted you and assure the crowd that you have the situation under control.

Although interruptions from the audience can be regarded as normal, the organisers of the event (perhaps the emcee) must be able to step in and handle the situation if there is an uncontrollable situation; for example, if there is a heated argument caused by members of the audience. In other cases, the speaker must be able to manage his audience well. A rule of thumb is that if one person asks a question, this means that four or five other audience members in the crowd had that question in mind but did not have the courage to interrupt the speaker. There are also times when the disruption may not even be audible. If might be a hand in the air or a facial expression that is clearly communicating the need to interact with you. As a speaker, observe these responses and reactions and attend to them accordingly.

The more you can maintain composure and approach the questions from the audience, the more confidence they will have in you. Do not be afraid to say, 'That is an outstanding question which is right here on my outline, and I will be answering that in a moment.' When you say something like this, it sets a lighter mood, and the person/people asking the question/s will appreciate the acknowledgement.

Be prepared to receive questions that you do not have answers for or questions that do not make any sense. What you need to do is to first acknowledge the question and then state that you will do some research and get back to them later with that background information.

Questions are not the only thing that can go wrong. Consider these scenarios: You accidentally drop your drinking glass, and it breaks. An audience member trips over her skirt when walking to the microphone and falls down. Or a bird could fly in through an open window. The list of unexpected things that could happen during a live event goes on and on.

Once again, as with the questions that you did not expect from the audience, the most important thing here is to maintain composure and control. The audience reacts to your actions, and when you unnecessarily panic, they might panic too. However, if you keep your cool and handle the disruption/interruption with calmness, or perhaps humour (if it does not embarrass your audience, of course!), that will put the audience in the same light mood too. The effects of the disruption/interruption will immediately minimise, and you will retain the audience's focus throughout the rest of your presentation.

You can achieve a feeling of calmness and being in control by thinking through how you will handle any unexpected situation before stepping up in front of your audience to speak. When you can actually expect the unexpected, you will be able to demonstrate a better understanding of your audience's expectations and have better management of time when you speak. This works to your advantage, and you will undoubtedly achieve the desired outcomes.

CHAPTER 10

Conclusion

Before we conclude, shall I start with a recap of the earlier chapters?

We understand now for a fact that knowing the basics on the fear of public speaking can help us overcome the anxiety and worry associated with it. But simply knowing about it is not enough. Acting on it should be the priority. That way, you will be taking the actual step towards improving your communication skills and eventually achieving your dreams of becoming a highly-impactful speaker and presenter.

What do you have in mind when I say that someone is brave? I believe you will think that I am referring to a category of people who are fearless, full of life, and have the courage to pursue something better because they believe in their purpose. As human beings, it is normal for us to have fears, but what differentiates one from the other is the courage to face the fear itself. This is also true in the case of public speaking. Whilst it may be natural for some to speak in public, others might not share the same sentiment.

If you are in the latter category, this book is especially written for you.

At all times, remind yourself that you are not alone in this fear. The only real difference is how different people react differently. One of the reasons why there is a difference could be due to the person's background or the person's experiences going through life.

You may be a shy and reserved person or someone quite the opposite. You may have natural speaking talents or otherwise. Regardless of your background and character, I hope that after reading this book, you will be able to improve your communication skills and, ultimately, transform you in your quest towards becoming a high-impact speaker and presenter.

In the previous chapters, I have shared my ABC Method, which consists of three principles that I have practised all this time—aspiration, behaviour, and connection. I firmly believe that these principles of high-impact speaking and presenting will work for you as much as they had worked for me.

Every time I speak and conduct presentations to different sets of audience, I observed that these principles had helped me in my speech and presentation delivery. This has brilliantly worked for me throughout my over 20 years of experience in various industries. Of course, the secret here is in the amount of consistent practice.

But before everything else even takes place, you must start by having clarity. In this context, having clarity means having the ability to define yourself, i.e., who you are and what you aspire to be.

What is the meaning of life without a clear and definite purpose? This is why I placed aspiration as the first principle in my ABC Method. Having clarity is extremely essential to ensure that you are able to achieve the goals that you have identified in life. Once you have it, your life aspirations are clear, and you will be able to overcome the challenges that may impede your journey. It enables you to organise your thoughts in a structured manner and make the necessary preparations prior to speaking and presenting in front of an audience.

The second principle that I spoke about relates to the way we conduct ourselves when we speak in public, which is behaviour. I mentioned in an earlier chapter that when we speak of a person's behaviour whilst speaking or presenting to an audience, two critical ingredients must be observed, which include the person's self-presentation and delivery methods.

Good speakers attempt to present themselves to shape their audience's view of them; therefore, they pay detailed attention in their appearance and personality. I have observed how many speakers fail to see the importance of this. For example, they may have a well-prepared presentation on personal grooming; however, they appear on stage sloppily dressed. Imagine the kind of impression they must have created on their audience!

High-impact behaviour produces an effective and persuasive action so that you may have full control of yourself. Consequently, you will accomplish a high level of confidence, which inevitably reduces your anxiety level.

Once you have this in place, the next important principle is connection. Connection refers to the actions that bind and unite you with your audience. It is about how you engage and maintain strong engagement with your audience throughout your performance. Bear in mind that when we speak to other people, we are connected with them in various ways in that particular moment in time, which means that in the course of our speech or presentation, we have indirectly created a trust level with our audience.

Now that you fully understand the ABC Method and how you need to master each principle before making your appearance on stage, the next step is to develop a personal approach that works best for you.

Notwithstanding this, adapting the personal development plans of others could work for you, but along the way, you will realise that you will be most comfortable following a plan, which is fluid enough for you, to move forward in your journey towards becoming a highly-impactful speaker and presenter.

As each person has unique experiences and associations, it is always best to cater to an approach that works for you; therefore, you need to put aside some time to really think about how to set powerful public speaking goals that are applicable to you.

The personal development plan template that I have shared with you in the earlier chapter is a basic plan that identifies your public speaking goals, what actions you need to take to achieve each goal, what resources you might need in the process, and a status column which shows your current progress for each goal. Remember, your personal development plan is a dynamic document that needs to be reviewed time and again to ensure that you are truly moving forward in achieving your goals.

As a final note from me, before you embark on your exciting journey to become a high-impact public speaker and presenter, at all times, always remember to enjoy the moment and have fun. Your positive attitude, the way you behave when you speak, and how you connect with the audience will all have a profound effect on them.

The audience needs to be able to feel your powerful energy. If your energy is low and you speak monotonously, they will easily lose interest. A topic can be dull and dreary, but the way you present adds colour to it. On the contrary, your topic might be extremely interesting, but you are unable to present it well, making the presentation a drag. The bottom line is you need to enjoy what you are talking about and inject passion and enthusiasm into your presentation. This is what I mean by having fun!

I have shared with you the ABC Method, which I believe will work for you like how it did for me. Getting the right balance amongst the three principles will work in the best of your favour.

To obtain maximum impact in the application of the ABC Method, adhering to the following steps is crucial towards ensuring a successful presentation:

 a. Prepare
 b. Practise
 c. Reflect

Prepare

Preparing for a presentation is undoubtedly a very important factor that could either make or break a presentation.

However, this step is often overlooked as some presenters feel that it is tedious or unnecessary or even a waste of time. Skipping through this step could be one of the presenter's biggest mistakes.

When you have prepared well, this ensures that you have carefully thought through the entire process of your presentation, which means that you are able to communicate key messages to your audience and convey significant takeaways that they should get from your presentation.

It is fundamental to have a checklist as preparation prior to presentation. The checklist should clearly state the purpose and expected outcome of the presentation, and going through the checklist well before your presentation starts will ensure nothing is missed.

Let me give you an example. Although a checklist item could be as simple as numbering your speaking notes, it could prove to be very useful if you accidentally drop your notes during your presentation because you will then be able to check the numbers and carry on with your presentation smoothly as opposed to scrambling to pick up the pieces of your notes on the floor whilst being watched by your audience. This would certainly create an awkward scene!

All items in the checklist should be thoroughly checked and confirmed that they are completed. Quality preparation is when another person runs through your checklist with you to ensure that nothing is missed. It is always advisable to get a fresh pair of eyes so that everything is complete before you start your presentation.

Practice

It is vital for you as a presenter to practise every single aspect of your presentation. Nothing should be regarded as too trivial.

A rehearsal is extremely important because it will provide you the opportunity to practise different parts of your presentation and work on your words, your angle, and your presenting style.

If something does not work, it allows you to substitute and/or revise texts that would effectively work back into your presentation. Prior to delivering in front of your audience, you are free to make edits on your speech and numerously rehearse until you get what you really wish to obtain.

My tip is to practise in front of a mirror so that you can see how you actually look when delivering your presentation. Perhaps you look a bit harsh when presenting; hence, you may need to soften your facial expressions to ensure that your audience feels comfortable throughout your presentation. The last thing you need is to create an unpleasant situation amongst your audience!

It also helps to record yourself during these practice rounds so that you can play back the audio and/or video for self-evaluation purposes. By doing this, you can focus on your strengths whilst at the same making improvements on your shortcomings.

Make an effort to have a guide; for example, numbered cards or short notes to facilitate the delivery of your presentation.

Reflect

If you look back on your presentation and the preparation that you have taken before presenting to your audience, you will be amazed to see how much you have learnt from the process.

A good idea is to list out your 'feel good' moments—for example, the interest they had shown on some of the issues you raised—and also the 'not so good' moments—for example, their confusion on some of the recommendations that you had proposed. All these could be based on your own observations or what you personally feel or it could even be feedback from others who witnessed your presentation.

It is a good habit to reflect on different parts of your presentation to see how you could have done it better and how you can improve it for your future presentations.

Always start with a dream and put aside the fear that you have inside of you. It's now time for you to go ahead and live your dream. I am already living mine.

You have escaped the cage. Your wings are stretched out. Now fly.
—Rumi

www.ingramcontent.com/pod-product-compliance
Lightning Source LLC
Chambersburg PA
CBHW030742180526
45163CB00003B/897